John Ackerman ('that brilliant commentator' wrote Andrew Sinclair) is a Welshman from Maesteg – a town ten miles or so to the east of Swansea, Thomas's birthplace. He thereby shares with the poet those literary, religious and social traditions which enable a Welshman to say of Dylan – after the briefest experience of his work – 'He is one of us'. John Ackerman's earlier volume *Dylan Thomas: His Life and Work* (O.U.P. 1964) was widely and enthusiastically reviewed. The present work is a distillation of that book, with important new material on the poetry and *Under Milk Wood* and new photographs.

Also by John Ackerman

Dylan Thomas: His Life and Work
The Image and the Dark (*Poems*)

Plate 1. Dylan as a child.

John Ackerman

Welsh Dylan

Dylan Thomas's Life, Writing, and his Wales

A PALADIN BOOK

GRANADA

London Toronto Sydney New York

Published by Granada Publishing Limited
in 1980

ISBN 0 586 08350 2

First published by John Jones Ltd 1979

The author and publishers gratefully acknowledge the permission granted to them by the Trustees for the Copyrights of the late Dylan Thomas, and by J. M. Dent & Sons Ltd., to quote extensively from Dylan Thomas's work and letters.
Thanks are also due to the Welsh Arts Council for their assistance.

The publishers wish to thank the following from whose collections photographs have been reproduced:
Pamela Hansford Johnson, plates 17 and 35; David Higham Associates Limited and the State University of New York at Buffalo, plate 19; David Higham Associates Limited, plate 52; Mrs Rollie McKenna, plates 20, 30, 42, 45; Aerofilms Ltd., plate 46; courtesy of the Welsh Arts Council and National Library of Wales, Aberystwyth, plate 55; unknown, plates 1, 3, 4, 12, 14, 23, 24, 44, 47, 48, 54, 56, 57; all contemporary photographs by John Idris Jones.
The publishers have made every endeavour to trace the copyright holders of the unknown plates.

Picture research by Angela Laycock

Granada Publishing Limited
Frogmore, St Albans, Herts AL2 2NF
and
3 Upper James Street, London W1R 4BP
866 United Nations Plaza, New York, NY 10017, USA
117 York Street, Sydney, NSW 2000, Australia
100 Skyway Avenue, Rexdale, Ontario, M9W 3A6, Canada
PO Box 84165, Greenside, 2034 Johannesburg, South Africa
61 Beach Road, Auckland, New Zealand

Filmset in 'Monophoto' Ehrhardt 10 on 12 pt and
printed in Great Britain by
Fletcher & Son Ltd, Norwich

Contents

This book is dedicated to the memory of my mother, whose generosity enabled me to undertake my first research on Dylan Thomas and whose interest always sustained.

Preface

The twenty-five years that have passed since his death have seen the acceptance of Dylan Thomas as a major twentieth-century poet. Likewise, knowledge of the Welsh background is now a *sine qua non* of serious Dylan Thomas criticism. Inevitably, and I think properly, *Welsh Dylan* has grown from my continuing work on the poet over these years, in books, articles, and reviews. While *Welsh Dylan* largely incorporates the view of the poet presented in *Dylan Thomas: His Life and Work*, particularly the importance of the Welsh background, it also draws on Thomas's letters and manuscript material, not available when I wrote my first book, to illuminate the poet's life and writing. Consequently I have given some attention to the growth of the poet and the emergence of his unique style. Additionally, my recent research has clarified for me the fundamental role of nature in Thomas's work, and *Welsh Dylan* explores this. It explores, too, the evidence of Thomas's development in new directions as poet and dramatist in his last years, throwing new light on *Under Milk Wood* and the last poems. It is a view of Thomas contrary to the falsifying legend of failing inspiration. With the help of photographs of places and settings that inspired him and fruitfully directed his imagination, *Welsh Dylan* follows the life of a lyric poet who celebrated the distinctive worlds of his childhood, adolescence and manhood with undiminished passion and energy. Finally, I have examined the problem of the lyric poet passionately learning to grow old. Throughout, my interest has not been to sensationalize the life, but to relate the man and the work. It is a continuing attempt to discover, and where possible to elucidate, his side of the truth.

John Ackerman,
Senior Lecturer in English,
Avery Hill College,
April 1979.

PART I

Swansea and the early years: 1914–1934: Growth of the Poet

'One: I am a Welshman; two: I am a drunkard; three: I am a lover of the human race, especially of women.'[1] This concise, humorous, and not untruthful account of himself is Dylan's own. Interestingly Dylan Thomas put his Welsh identity first, for these were days before national feeling strongly flavoured the culture and thought of English-speaking Welshmen. Undoubtedly Dylan Thomas's poetry and prose has uniquely drawn the world's attention to Wales: his Swansea stories, his Laugharne-charted poems, his glimpses of Eden and of eternity in the landscapes of West Wales, and *Under Milk Wood*'s evocations of warm, gossiping incorrigibly human Welsh life have captivated the popular as well as the literary imagination of the second half of the twentieth century. Of course Wales is a country of those two languages so richly endowed with poetry, Welsh and English, and though the dragon speaks with two tongues it is Wales he speaks of.

'This sea town was my world'[2] wrote Dylan Thomas of Swansea, where he was born in 1914, and it was with a cannily prophetic note that the poet Edward Thomas, himself of Welsh origins, remarked of Swansea: 'If Wales could produce a poet he should be born in the hills and come here at the age of sixteen. He would have no need of Heaven and Hell.'[3] On another occasion Edward Thomas speaks of Swansea as that 'horrible and sublime town'[3] and observes that 'it is very large . . . it is all furnaces, collieries, filth, stench, poverty and extravagant show, the country and the sea at the very edge of it all.' How similar this is to Dylan Thomas's 'I was born in a large Welsh industrial town at the beginning of the Great War: an ugly lovely town (or so it was, and is, to me), crawling, sprawling, slummed, unplanned, jerryvilla'd, and smug-suburbed by the side of a long and splendid-curving shore'.[4] Both writers remark upon the close proximity of industry, the countryside, and the sea – a familiar feature of South Wales. And Swansea provided a vivid theatre of Welsh life: for it was a seaside resort, a shopping centre with its inviting market of such local produce as laverbread and

Plate 2. No. 5, Cwmdonkin Drive.

cockles from near-by Penclawdd, Carmarthenshire butter, bacon, eggs, and poultry; it was the scene, too, of rugby, football, and cricket matches and provider of the varied and colourful pubs of a dockside, holiday resort and commercial town. It was a Welsh mecca for day-trippers from the surrounding valleys:

Never was there such a town (I thought) for the smell of fish and chips on Saturday nights, for the Saturday afternoon cinema matinées where we shouted and hissed our threepences away; for the crowds in the streets, with leeks in their pockets, on international nights, for the singing that gushed from the smoking doorways of the pubs.[2]

In later years, remembering his childhood in the town Dylan spoke of the Mumbles 'and the trains that hissed like ganders took us all to the beautiful beach';[4] and he mockingly recalled 'The museum, which should have been in a museum'.[2]

Dylan was born on 27 October 1914 in no. 5 Cwmdonkin Drive, a street 'up the uplands' and overlooking Swansea bay. His own upbringing belonged to suburban Swansea and enjoyed financial security, for his father was Senior English master at Swansea Grammar School during the period of social strife and deprivation that followed the First World War in industrial South Wales – 'outside (Swansea) a *strange* Wales, coal-pitted, mountained, river run, full, so far as I knew, of choirs and sheep!'[2] Writing to Pamela Hansford Johnson in 1933 Dylan humorously declares that

I first saw the light of day in a Glamorgan villa, and, amidst the terrors of the Welsh accent and the smoke of the tinplate stacks, grew up to be a sweet baby, a precocious child, a rebellious boy, and a morbid youth. My father was a schoolmaster: a broader-minded man I have never known. My mother came from the agricultural depths of Carmarthenshire.[5]

Undoubtedly Dylan was spoilt and pampered by his mother, who in later years recalled an argument with him over his refusal to attend to his studies at school:

'I said, "You know, you must try and get into the University – what are you going to do? Anybody'd think you were a Keats or something!" He looked at me – and he wasn't the cheeky type, he wasn't even a big talker – and he said, "I'll be as good as Keats, if not better." I went to his father and I said, "I'll never tell him anything again." '[6]

Undoubtedly, too, Dylan owed much more to his father's patient tutelage than to formal schooling, a debt of which he was aware. He spent much of his time in his father's study, which was particularly

Plate 3. Old view of Mumbles pier.

*Plate 4. D. J. Thomas,
Dylan's father.*

rich in its collection of English literature, and he left us this description
of their shared books:

Our books we divided into two sections, Dad's and mine. Dad has a room full
of all the accepted stuff, from Chaucer to Henry James, all the encyclopaedias
and books of reference, all Saintsbury, and innumerable books on the theory of
literature. His library contains nearly everything that a respectable highbrow
library should contain. My books, on the other hand, are nearly all poetry, and
mostly modern at that. I have the collected poems of Manley Hopkins, Stephen
Crane, Yeats, de la Mare, Osbert Sitwell, Wilfred Owen, W. H. Auden, and T.
S. Eliot, volumes of poetry by Aldous Huxley, Sacheverell and Edith Sitwell,
Edna St. Vincent Millay, D. H. Lawrence, Humbert Woolf, Sassoon, and
Harold Monro; most of the ghastly Best Poems of the Year; two of the Geor-
gian Anthologies, one of the Imagist anthologies, 'Whips & Scorpions' (modern
satiric verse), the London Mercury Anthology, the Nineties Anthology (what
Dowsonery!), most of Lawrence, most of Joyce, with the exception of Ulysses, all

Gilbert Murray's Greek translations, some Shaw, a little Virginia Woolf, and some of E. M. Forster. This is inadequate really, but added to Dad's it makes a really comprehensive selection of literature.[7]

I have quoted at length since, as later excerpts from the school magazine that Thomas edited and contributed to will corroborate, he was by no means the wild untutored youth his own recollected accounts of his childhood are apt to suggest. By adolescence he was a very knowledgeable and informed 'Rimbaud of Cwmdonkin Drive!'[8]

Both Dylan Thomas's parents spoke Welsh, and both had their roots in rural West Wales. Interestingly D. J. Thomas, who graduated in English from the University College of Aberystwyth in 1899, was noted in Swansea Grammar School for his enthusiastic and impassioned reading of English literature, a gift his son evidently inherited. No doubt, too, it was his father who took the name Dylan from its source in the Mabinogion:

And they brought her unto him, and the maiden came in. 'Ha, damsel,' said he, 'art thou a maiden?' 'I know not lord, other than that I am.' Then he took up his magic wand, and bent it. 'Step over this,' said he, 'and I shall know if thou art the maiden.' Then stepped she over the magic wand, and there appeared forthwith a fine chubby yellow-haired boy! . . .

'Verily,' said Math the son of Mathonwy, concerning the fine yellow-haired boy. 'I will cause this one to be baptized, and Dylan is the name I will give him.'

Plate 5. Maen Dylan – the Rock of Dylan – on the coast west of Caernarfon.

So they had the boy baptized, and as they baptized him he plunged into the sea. And immediately when he was in the sea, he took its nature, and swam as well as the best fish that was therein. And for that reason was he called Dylan, the son of the Wave.[9]

Dylan comments on the source and pronunciation of his name in a letter to Pamela Hansford Johnson that 'my unusual name, for some mad reason, it comes from the Mabinogion ... rhymes with Chillun'.[10]

Dylan's middle name Marlais has an equally interesting derivation, for it celebrates the notable Welsh poet, preacher, and radical, William Thomas, who was the brother of Dylan's paternal grandfather. He wrote under the name of Gwilym Marles; he came from North Carmarthen, and Marlais is the name of a small river in this part of Carmarthenshire, whence he took this assumed 'bardic' name. Gwilym Marles became a Unitarian minister in Cardiganshire, writing both poetry and prose in Welsh. He was especially famous for his radicalism, being a liberal in theology and a radical in politics; he and his congregation were evicted from the chapel by the local landowner. He is included in the *Oxford Book of Welsh Verse*, and his career is an interesting example of the way in which Nonconformist, radical, and popular sympathies in Welsh life tend to unite. Dylan's mother, Florence Thomas, a deacon's daughter, came from the poorer industrial part of Swansea, though her family too had its roots in Carmarthenshire farming country – indeed her sister Ann married Jim Jones who farmed 'Fern Hill'. This farm provides the setting for Dylan Thomas's most famous poem, and also the location of the story *The Peaches*; while Ann is commemorated in Thomas's finest early poem *After the Funeral*. Clearly then, Dylan Thomas's background was pedagogic, religious in the Nonconformist style with a strong emphasis on the individual conscience and the primacy of each man's knowledg of his Bible; and it was an upbringing with close roots in the rural life of West Wales. Dylan, his mother, and his sister Nancy, all attended the Paraclete Congregational Church, Newton, Mumbles, where his uncle – this time on the mother's side of the family – David Rees was minister. Here Dylan received the 'Sunday School Certificate I was ashamed to want to pull down'.[11]

Bordering Thomas's home in Cwmdonkin Drive was Cwmdonkin Park 'and the park itself was a world within a world of the sea town'[2] wrote the poet. It played a major role in his imaginative recreations of

Plate 6. Cwmdonkin Park.

childhood, as it had at the time of his actual childhood been a place of endless mystery, delight, and pleasure:

that small interior world widened as I learned its names and its boundaries, as I discovered new refuges and ambushes in its miniature woods and jungles, hidden homes and lairs for the multitudes of the young, for cowboys and Indians.

Dylan's nostalgia for the safe, bright, childhood world of the park illuminates his prose reminiscences:

I carried a wooden rifle in Cwmdonkin Park and shot down the invisible unknown enemy like a flock of wild birds . . . Though it was only a little park, it held within its borders old tall trees, notched with our names and shabby from our climbing, as many secret places, caverns and forests, prairies and deserts, as a country somewhere at the end of the sea.

Clearly the Park had its own, never-to-be-forgotten resonances in the growth of the poet's mind, offering a small but immediate natural world that nourished that combination of the strongly physical and deeply imaginative use of language that was always to characterize Thomas's writing. The poem *The Hunchback in the Park* derives its inspiration from Thomas's haunted and haunting memories of the place, and is an early example of how the poet makes direct use of particular Welsh landscapes; for the loved and familiar scene becomes the object around which his ideas evolve, so that we see and hear the solitary hunchback against that flowing childhood world of trees and water, a flux where the bell at dusk chimes with an echoing and sombre note before the dark that is to take away all this life and delight. We see here the children filling the chained cup with gravel, Dylan sailing ships in the fountain basin, the hunchback eating bread, drinking water from the chained cup:

> The hunchback in the park
> A solitary mister
> Propped between trees and water
> From the opening of the garden lock
> That lets the trees and water enter
> Until the Sunday sombre bell at dark
>
> Eating bread from a newspaper
> Drinking water from the chained cup
> That the children filled with gravel
> In the fountain basin where I sailed my ship
> Slept at night in a dog kennel
> But nobody chained him up.

Plate 7. The fountain in the park.

The selected detail is commonplace: it is Thomas's command of rhythm and image that is the controlling energy of the poem, the form inextricably part of the emotional life the poem records; so much so that it brings to mind the poet's defence of the form of another 'Cwmdonkin Poem' (*Once it was the colour of saying*) where he asserts that 'the form was consistently emotional and I can't change it without a change of heart'.[12]

In this poem compassion for the hunchback with his dream of

> A woman figure without fault
> Straight as a young elm

and who survives the coming dark, is linked with a nostalgia for the poet's own youth when 'the groves were blue with sailors' and 'the wild boys innocent as strawberries'. Interestingly the phrase 'blue with sailors' links two images, both the sailors to be seen in this dockside town and the park's bluebells, sometimes referred to as 'sailors' trousers' no doubt due to the shape and colour of the flower. In the latter 'strawberry' image we have the poet's favoured device of the transferred epithet (readers will recall the more familiar 'wild strawberries' and 'innocent boys') as a means of revitalizing the language, so that the lines become charged with new poetic life.

Comparison of the early version of this poem (9 May 1932), and the final version (16 July 1941), which was copied into the same notebook, shows how in later years Thomas sometimes drew his initial inspiration from an early notebook poem, though, as here, the final poem was virtually a new composition. Interestingly, Thomas replaces the South Wales word 'mitching' ('the mitching boys') with the more generally familiar 'truant' (both words have the same meaning), though he may also have been influenced by the fact that truant is more resonant in this context and is slightly echoed in 'town' at the end of the line. Significantly, the first manuscript version has the phrase 'Running . . . on out of sight';[13] the reader will appreciate how much more evocative and 'alive' in terms of sound and sight is the later 'on out of sound' for we now see and hear the boys disappear in this poem that is full of sound and movement as well as visual life. Effectively, too, they disappear more gradually; from sound then sight. Such verbal and imaginative devices are close to what is most distinctive and original in a poem by Dylan Thomas. Dr Daniel Jones, Thomas's boyhood friend, has said that 'There was indeed, a hunchback who seemed to have nowhere else to go, who stayed from the moment the park opened until it closed. Cwmdonkin Park was a favourite haunt for truants from Swansea Grammar School . . . Thomas and I often met there to read poems to one another or write them, when, perhaps, we should have been learning geography. But usually our amusements were more boisterous and less "cultured".'[14]

Dylan Thomas was a pupil at Swansea Grammar School from September 1925 until July 1931, 'the school he knew and loved when he was a boy up to no good but the beat of his blood'.[15] It seems Dylan took little interest in any subject except English, and enjoyed a somewhat privileged position regarding his neglect of other subjects, due to the fearsome presence of his father in the staffroom. Such stories abound as that telling of the occasion when he was stopped on leaving the school in early afternoon by the Headmaster, who asked, 'Where are you going?' 'Home to write poems,' replied Dylan. 'Well, don't get caught', said the Headmaster. Such a story probably accurately reflects Dylan's rather spoilt and privileged schoolboy existence. However, as well as his ability as a long-distance runner (he won the mile race in 1926), Dylan's contributions to school life lay in his work on the school magazine and in the school's Dramatic Society. It was Dylan's father who was responsible for the first issue of the magazine in the Christmas term 1903. Dylan edited the magazine, initially as co-editor, from December 1929 to July 1931. He contributed in his first term at school *The Song of the Mischievous Dog* – his first published poem. What is noticeable about his contributions to the school magazine is the large amount of parody and humorous verse. Throughout his life Thomas maintained, both in his writing and especially in his talk, this liking for parody and humour. The following example of his early parody is entitled *Children's Hour (or Why the B.B.C. Broke Down)* and was written when he was sixteen. It is an effective satire on the old Children's Hour style and was written as early as 1930.

(Aunt Fanny is conducting an excursion into Arcadia. Imagine her voice to be high-pitched, mellow, and very endearing . . .)

A.F.: Shall I transport you into the sylvan realms of Arcady, children, where the spring is twice as long as any other season, and where nymphs and shepherds, to say nothing of the dryads and other woodland denizens who infest the groves, dance, or rather frolic, for their dancing conforms to no ball-room regulations, the whole day through? Take my hand, then – no not that one, the clean one – Come let us away. (Here several uncles make loud hissing sounds between their teeth, and a small boy, who seems bored with the whole proceedings, bangs a drum) . . . Come, children, let us away, after having enjoyed a real spot of Arcadia. (The boy bangs the drum and goes home.) Come to the studio once more. Many happy returns to John Brown on his seventy-second birthday.'[16]

An article on modern poetry written in 1929 shows that at the age of 15 Thomas was a competent critic, with a remarkable knowledge of both contemporary and earlier English poetry and some felicity in critical expression. School magazine photographs show Dylan Thomas in the production of Drinkwater's *Abraham Lincoln* and in Galsworthy's *Strife*. Reviews of the plays performed also throw an interesting light on Dylan Thomas as a schoolboy, for we learn that 'D.M. Thomas gave a very good performance as Oliver Cromwell, in spite of the fact that physically he was not up to the part . . . he looked as young and as fresh and clean as if he had just come off the cover of a chocolate box.'[17] In similar vein we are told of *Strife* that 'D.M. Thomas had a most difficult task. There are times when he seemed to lack the coarseness and toughness of fibre necessary for the interpretation of Roberts (the strike leader); his vowels were occasionally too genteel!'[18] Interestingly, under the heading 'Things we cannot credit' in another number of the magazine is listed 'That D.M.T. should mispronounce a word'.[19] References to Thomas in the school magazine consistently offer the picture of a delicate, precocious, humorous, but essentially serious-minded boy.

Dylan Thomas left school in July 1931, having passed no major examinations, to work on the *South Wales Daily Post*, a position he held for a year and a half. It was a time of rapid development, for as a reporter his knowledge of life was greatly extended, and during this period he started drinking. It seems he was an indifferent reporter, and spent most of his days strolling about Swansea, gossiping and arguing the toss with friends, meeting people in pubs and cafés. He has given a humorous and vivid picture of himself:

A chap called Young Thomas. He worked on the *Post* and used to wear an overcoat sometimes with the check lining inside out so that you could play giant draughts on him. He wore a conscious Woodbine too.[20]

More serious and more revealing of the growth of the poet's mind and compassionate imagination is this earlier recollection from the story 'Old Garbo'; for it shows how his experience as a journalist was turning his eye outward to other people – a faculty exercised at first only in his prose writing – and he was observing the many-faceted, lively Swansea scenes with realism and accuracy, yet all the time aware of himself as the artist who would later create from this world the dramatic and richly human life of his stories:

I made my way through the crowds: the valley men, up for the football; the country shoppers; the window gazers; the silent, shabby men at the corners of the packed streets, standing in isolation in the rain; the press of mothers and prams; old women in black, broached dresses carrying frails; smart girls with shiny mackintoshes and splashed stockings; little, dandy lascars bewildered by the weather . . . and all the time I thought of the paragraphs I would never write. I'll put you all in a story by and by.

Now he was receiving his impressions of Swansea's microcosm of Welsh life; later he was to turn these experiences to his needs as a writer. The reference to 'silent, shabby men at corners . . . standing in isolation in the rain' are reminders – to us and the poet – that this was one of the bitter years of depression in Wales. Though not a political writer, Dylan remained steadily and – unlike some of his English contemporaries such as Auden – steadfastly on the left. Welsh radicalism, albeit more the child of nonconformity than Karl Marx, left its impact on the young poet. Dylan Thomas's political commitment to the left

24

owed little to the intellectual fashions of the thirties; deriving from his experiences in Swansea and the traditions of his Welsh environment, it was less ostentatious than that of contemporary English writers, though more enduring. He was reported in the *Strand* magazine to have said in March 1947, during the winter freeze-up and fuel crisis that hit the post-war Labour government, 'One should tolerate the Labour Government because running down Labour eventually brings you alongside the Conservatives, which is the last place you want to be!'

During his time as journalist Thomas wrote many articles of literary interest which contain a good deal of remote and scholarly material. It is clear that he went to great pains in securing his information. The articles are factual rather than interpretative. They deal with the lives and work of local poets and with the visits of such celebrities as Landor, Borrow, and Edward Thomas to Swansea. Like Thomas's reviews in the *Adelphi*, written in his early twenties, they reveal unexpected erudition and critical judgement, showing that he brought considerable seriousness of purpose to more local fields of interest. They represent a less familiar part of his many-sided personality and one unfortunately that has tended to be forgotten in the falsifying light of the later legend. This almost scholarly aspect of himself he was disinclined to include in his public personality. It is from this vein of dedication to detail that flows the complete absorption in craftsmanship that marks his growth as a poet and prose writer.

In these articles Thomas had some incisive things to say about Welshmen writing poetry in English:

It is curious that the wonders of Celtic mythology, and the inexplicable fascination that Welsh legends are bound to exercise upon whoever takes enough trouble to become acquainted with them, have not influenced the Anglo-Welsh poets more considerably. W. H. Davies, the most gifted Welsh poet writing in English today, could, if he had chosen, have made something very great out of the legends of his own country. He could have recreated the fantastic world of the Mabinogion, surrounded the folklore with his own fancies, and made his poetry a stepping-place for the poor children of darkness to reach a saner world where the cancer of our warped generation is no more than a pleasant itch.

But he preferred to follow in the direct line of the hedgerow poets, leaning over some country stile with placid expression, thinking of nothing more edifying than the brevity of life, the green of the grass, and the inanity of personal expression.

There is a caustic note in this criticism of W. H. Davies, and one recalls how much more profound, original, complex to the point of obscurity, was Dylan Thomas's own wrestling with the themes of

Plate 8. View of Swansea from Cwmdonkin Drive.

mutability in man and nature; and how striking was the expression of
vitality and wonder of the natural world in his own poetry at this time.
What the article reveals, too, is that Thomas was giving thought to the
relationship between the Anglo-Welsh writer and his inherited Welsh
literary tradition, and also of course to the problems that confronted the
writer in the present in Wales – for Thomas powerfully concludes:

> Only a great writer can give this absurd country, full of green fields, and chim-
> ney stacks, beauty and disease, the loveliness of the villages and the smoke-
> ridden horror of the towns, its full value and recognition.[21]

Value and recognition were certainly what Dylan Thomas was to give
to the land and seascapes, the traditions and life of South and West
Wales.

At this time Dylan found that the pub was his natural background,
the place to meet people and to talk and also to listen – for he was a
good listener. The pub, too, provided the sounding board for his wit,
was where good talk could flow as easily as the beer, and where opening
hours provided easy, convivial company, pals ever ready to exchange
the tall story, the ribald joke, the delightful item of news or gossip
concerning the weird vagaries of human nature: and here, too, beery
fantasy kept at bay the outside world. In *Return Journey* Thomas re-

called, in his search for the past Swansea boy, 'he used to work as a reporter. Down "The Three Lamps" I used to see him lifting his ikkle elbow.' These were, too, the rebellious years of adolescence, and marked out by the accusing finger of Welsh nonconformity no artist could feel more of a young dog than Dylan Thomas in Swansea. Yet, though defiant and aiming to shock, there was always an element of guilt lurking behind the bravado, as in this later description of the young reporter's initiation into the drinking scene:

The back room of 'The Three Lamps' was full of elderly men. Mr Farr had not arrived. I leaned against the bar, between an alderman and a solicitor, drinking bitter, wishing that my father could see me now and glad at the same time that he was visiting Uncle A. in Aberavon. He could not fail to see that I was a boy no longer, nor fail to be angry at the angle of my fag and my hat and the threat of the clutched tankard.[22]

Dylan was now a member of Swansea Little Theatre, and his acting roles included Simon Bliss in Coward's *Hay Fever*, Count Bellair in Farquhar's *The Beaux' Stratagem*, and Witwoud in *The Way of the World*. Undoubtedly acting was one of his deepest interests and pleasures, though *en route* for rehearsals at the Little Theatre he was apt to be delayed by visits to two of his favourite Mumbles pubs 'The Mermaid' and 'The Antelope' which he fondly referred to as 'these two legendary creatures'.[23] Writing to his friend Trevor Hughes in 1932 he

Plate 9. The Mermaid, Mumbles.

Plate 10. The Antelope.

complains of a hangover after a drinking session in Mumbles with Dan Jones, 'Oh, woe, woe, woe unto Mumbles and the oystered beer.'[24] In a letter written shortly before this the poet boasts how, despite the pressures of his job as a reporter, the demands of rehearsals, and of the Muse, he manages several nights' drinking each week:

I am playing in Noel Coward's *Hay Fever* at the Little Theatre this season. Much of my time is taken up with rehearsals. Much is taken up with concerts, deaths, meetings and dinners. It's odd, but between all these I manage to become drunk at least four nights of the week. Muse or Mermaid?

Thomas's description of drinking a pint of beer has the physical immediacy, the vivid directness, the movement, colour and imaginative opening out of the experience that is characteristic of his best writing. It is above all an inviting description:

I liked the taste of beer, its live, white lather, its brass-bright depths, the sudden world through the wet brown walls of the glass, the tilted rush to the lips and the slow, swallowing down to the lapping belly, the salt on the tongue, the foam at the corners.[22]

The letters Dylan wrote at this time (1932–34) evoke perhaps the most illuminating and detailed picture of his daily life, and of his thoughts on and reactions to the world around him, that we have. As well as providing, like the letters of Keats, fascinating glimpses of the growth of the young poet's mind and sensibility, they reveal Thomas's concern with such matters as religious experience, politics, and sexuality, and explain the outline concepts and attitudes he was to keep the kernel of for the rest of his life. In a letter to Pamela Hansford Johnson, October 1933, the poet describes his day, beginning with his waking moments, then breakfast of 'an apple, an orange, and a banana' and a read of the newspaper in bed. Downstairs, seated before the fire he begins two hours' reading 'anything that is near, poetry or prose, translations out of the Greek or the Film Pictorial, a new novel . . . a new book of criticism, or an old favourite like Grimm or George Herbert'.[25] What is clear is that Thomas's reading was voracious, casual, varied, and a matter of total absorption. There was little that was prescribed, deliberate, planned; it was essentially that of the autodidact and chameleon imagination. Soon after midday a walk to the nearby Uplands Hotel for a couple of pints of beer, then home for lunch and an afternoon's reading or writing – 'to write anything, just to let the words and ideas, the half-remembered half-forgotten images, tumble on the sheets of paper'. As was to be the case for most of Thomas's life it is a casual yet curiously regular and regulated routine.

Sometimes, we learn, he would 'spend the afternoon in walking alone over the very desolate Gower cliffs, communing with the cold and

Plate 11. The Uplands Hotel.

quietness. I call this taking my devils for an airing'. Young Dylan was deeply fond of the Gower coast and on another occasion he writes that 'I often go down in the mornings to the furthest point of Gower – the village of Rhossili – and stay there till evening. The bay is the wildest, bleakest & barrenest I know – four or five miles of yellow coldness going away into the distance of the sea.'[26] It is a camping holiday in Rhossili that is described in *Extraordinary Little Cough*, which opens 'one afternoon in a particularly bright and glowing August, some years before I knew I was happy'. This story was written in 1938, and follows the closely autobiographical pattern of the collection *Portrait of the Artist as a Young Dog*. Dylan called the stories 'illuminated reporting',[27] and though it is childhood and adolescent experience that preoccupies him there is not yet the consuming nostalgia, that desperate cry of Captain Cat in *Under Milk Wood* 'Come back, come back' that was to direct Thomas's later prose writing. His present and immediate rendering of experience in his letters often, as we shall see, provided an interesting contrast with the later recollected scenes and events. Warming to his present description of the Rhossili setting he describes The Worm's Head, Gower:

And the Worm, a seaworm of rock pointing into the channel, is the promontary of depression . . . When the tide comes in, the reef of needle rocks that leads to the base of the Worm, is covered under water. I was trapped on the Worm once. I had gone on it early in the afternoon with a book and a bag of food, and, going to the very, very end, had slept in the sun, with the gulls crying like mad over me. And when I woke the sun was going down. I ran over the rocks . . . The tide had come in. I stayed on that Worm from dusk to midnight, sitting on the top grass, frightened to go further in because of the rats and because of the things I am ashamed to be frightened of.[26]

Clearly such adventures fired the poet's imagination, for writing to his friend Trevor Hughes (also featured in these stories) a few months previously the setting provides a literary injunction:

Remember the Worm, read a meaning into its symbol, a serpent's head, rising out of the clean sea.[28]

The same imaginative power informs the description of a Whitsun visit to Laugharne in 1934 in the compay of his friend and fellow Anglo-Welsh writer Glyn Jones. 'I am a Symbol Simon,' Dylan declares self-mockingly, and then inventively and yet with realistic vigour relates his holiday scene on this 'hopeless fallen angel of a day'.[29]

The poetic and comic qualities in Thomas's prose writing were to remain, but in these letters we have a unique picture of the challenging,

Plate 12. Dylan and his mother on the Gower Cliffs.

Plate 13. Worm's Head, Gower

questioning, albeit anarchic, mind of Thomas in these years of late adolescence. His ideas on society would not easily fit a social framework – their very individuality and eloquence do not belong to the realm of practical application (as he is aware) – but it is a side and sight of the poet's thinking now largely forgotten or neglected in favour of the more superficially sensational aspects of his life and legendary personality. His views on adolescent sexuality would still be thought socially revolutionary:

From the first months of puberty girls and boys should be allowed to know their bodies ... More than that, their sexual expression should be encouraged. It would be very nearly impossible for a young girl to live, permanently, with a young boy, especially if both were in school; they would not live together peaceably; they would have no money, and it would be difficult for them to earn. But the family of the girl should for a certain time – the time of the mutual devotion of the boy and girl – keep the boy in their house. And vice-versa. The lives of the boy and girl would continue individually – there would be school and school associations for both of them – but their domestic closeness and their sleeping together would blend the two individual lives in one and would keep both brains and bodies perpetually clean.[30]

With similar eloquence, vigour, and social commitment Dylan Thomas writes on Armistice Day 1933 – he was then nineteen – in protest and anger against the still remembered griefs and anguish caused by the casualties of the First World War. His comments on the need for revolution are revealing not simply for what they say – for his idealism and iconoclasm are untempered by political experience – but primarily for the urgency and seriousness with which he is engaged with the subject:

This is written on Armistice Day, 1933, when the war is no more than a memory of privations and the cutting down of the young. There were women who had 'lost' their sons, though where they had lost them and why they could not find them, we, who were children born out of blood into blood, could never tell. The state was a murderer ... What was Christ in us was stuck with a bayonet to the sky, and what was Judas we fed and sheltered ... Genius is being strangled every day by the legion of old Buffers ... clinging, for God and capital, to an outgrown and decaying system. Light is being turned to darkness by the capitalists and industrialists. There is only one thing you and I, who are of this generation, must look forward to, must work for and pray for, and, because we are poets and voicers, not only of our personal selves but of our social selves, we must pray for ... It is the Revolution. There is no need for it to be a revolution of blood. We do not ask that ... we ask ... that all that is in us of godliness and strength, of happiness and genius, shall be allowed to exult in the sun. We are said to be faithless, because our God is not a capitalist God, to be unpatriotic because we do not believe in the Tory Government.[31]

We must remember of course that the year was 1933, a time of poverty for many and a time of social unrest, and that Thomas's voice is that of an idealistic, rebellious young man; but what has seldom been sufficiently realized is that the mind that produced the early, introspective, strikingly original but strongly solipsistic poetry was the product of a particular time and a particular place, a mind as informed and as socially aware as the more political and less subjective writers. Thomas is as dismissive of the churches as he is of Government and the press – and eloquently so, protesting that 'they standardize our Gods . . . label our morals . . . laud the death of a vanished Christ, and fear the crying of the new Christ in the wilderness.'

Thomas's life in Swansea at this time was well nourished by cultural and intellectual interests, for the town was a lively centre of artistic activity. Thomas's group of artist friends included the composer, Daniel Jones, and Alfred Janes, the painter. Their endless, adolescent discussions on 'music and poetry and painting and politics, Einstein

SWANSEA AND THE ARTS

RODUCED on the front page of the "Radio Times" th is week, this photograph, taken by an "Evening Post" pho ier, shows the five Swansea men who will take part in the programme, "Swansea and the Arts," at 8.30 p.m. on Mon ed round the table, left to right, are Vernon Watkins, John Pritchard, Alfred Janes, Daniel Jones and Dylan Thor in Thomas and Vernon Watkins are two of the foremost po ets in Europe. John Pritchard is an Atlantic Prize win se first novel will be published soon; Alfred Janes has he ld an exhibition of his paintings in Swansea and will be sho ing one in London; and Daniel Jones is the only Welsh co mposer to have written a symphony. He will conduct ion Philharmonic Orchestra in a performance of this wo rk on the Thursday night of the Swansea Festival. Stand is John Griffiths, who produces the programme.

Plate 14. 'Swansea and the Arts'.

and Epstein, Stravinsky and Greta Garbo, death and religion', Thomas fondly mocks in his *Return Journey* to the town years later. Their favourite meeting place was the Kardomah café. It was in conversations with Bert Trick, a grocer, and a man active in the local Labour Party as well as being interested in poetry, that no doubt Dylan's political ideas were stimulated. Other friends included Mervyn Levy, the painter, Wynford Vaughan-Thomas, the journalist and broadcaster, and of course Vernon Watkins, the fellow Swansea poet. It was on one of the recurrent return journeys to Swansea, after he had left for London, that Thomas first met Vernon Watkins. This group of Swansea friends was to remain a loyal, enduring company. Vernon Watkins, who was born in Maesteg, a mining town in the Llynfi valley, worked as a bank clerk in the St Helen's Road branch of Lloyd's in Swansea, and lived in Pennard, a particularly lovely coastal stretch of Gower. From the time of their first meeting the two poets discussed their work together, and their exchange of letters is a rare and fascinating commentary on the practice of poetry, especially for those interested in the process of poetic composition. Vernon Watkins relates how they became close friends almost immediately, each recognizing an affinity in their view of poetry, especially in the importance of reading it aloud. His picture of Dylan on their first meeting is a characteristically generous and perceptive one:

He was slight, shorter than I had expected, shy, rather flushed and eager in manner, deep-voiced, restless, humorous, with large wondering, yet acutely intelligent eyes, gold curls, snub nose and the face of a cherub. I quickly realised when we went for a walk on the (Gower) cliffs that this cherub took nothing for granted. In thought and words he was anarchic, challenging, with the certainty of that instinct which knows its own freshly discovered truth.[32]

Visually the description recalls Augustus John's portrait; the 'freshly discovered truth' brings to mind the striking originality of Thomas's first collection *18 Poems*. Thomas's own recollection of these Swansea days of warm friendships, shared ambitions, youthful confidence, is of course marked by that humour Vernon Watkins noted on their first meeting. Dylan records 'how Dan Jones was going to compose the most prodigious symphony, Fred Janes paint the most miraculously meticulous picture, Vernon Watkins and Young Thomas write the most boiling poems'.[33] At the time, however, Dylan was experiencing not only the social pleasures of Swansea but the loneliness of the artist, albeit with the bravado of the young dog. Visiting Swansea sands and fairground in summer, he was a poet in his isolation, but also 'a young man in a sea

Plate 15. Dylan's room in Cwmdonkin Drive.

town on a warm bank holiday, with two pounds to spend'.[34]

For perhaps the truest picture of Dylan in these years of late ado-
lescence we can turn to the later, closely autobiographical stories of *Por-
trait of the Artist as a Young Dog*, as the earlier ones accurately evoked
his childhood in Swansea and Fern Hill. Thus in *One Warm Saturday* 'the
young man, in his wilderness, saw the holiday Saturday set down before
him' on Swansea bay. Having declined his friends' invitation to a trip
to Porthcawl, now he 'thought of Porthcawl's Coney Beach, where his
friends were rocking with girls on the Giant racer or tearing in the
Ghost train'. Instead of enjoying these pleasures he 'stood listening to
Mr Matthews, the retired drinker, crying darkness on the evening
sands', though he characteristically observes that 'Boys with peashooters
sat quietly near him. A ragged man collected nothing in a cap.' During
the day the young poet has joined in a game of cricket with a family on
the sands, until a dog carries the ball into the sea and swims with it out

*Plate 16. 'Ghostly
Ebenezer Chapel'.*

of reach. 'All his friends had vanished into their pleasures' and the poet
mocks himself, poking fun at his self-pity and despair:

He thought: Poets live and walk with their poems; a man with visions needs no
other company . . . I must go home and sit in my bedroom by the boiler.

He meets a beautiful young woman, and after getting drunk accom-
panies her to a party. Finally, the poet makes his way home alone, the
end of the story suggesting man's continuing need for compassion and
fuller understanding – emotions rooted in Thomas's love for the 'ugly
lovely town':

Then he walked out . . . The light of the one weak lamp in a misty circle fell across the brick heaps and the broken wood and the dust that had been houses once, where the small and hardly known and never-to-be-forgotten people of the dirty town had lived and loved and died, and, always, lost.

This of course is the more serious side of the artist, no longer the young dog but the impassioned spokesman for his people. We catch something of the artist's isolation, albeit in these years linked with the isolation of the adolescent, in his account of night-time strolls in Swansea:

I was a lonely night-walker and a steady stander-at-corners, I liked to walk through the wet town . . . in dead and empty High Street under the moon, gigantically sad, in the damp streets by ghostly Ebenezer Chapel . . .

Something of this sense of isolation lies behind the steely dedication of the young Dylan to his vocation as a poet. For the important achievement of these years of adolescence in Swansea was the emergence of one of the most original poets to write in the English language. The evidence of this is contained in the notebooks of manuscript poems covering the years 1930–34, what Dylan called 'some of my innumerable exercise books'.[35] It was a period of energetic and fertile poetic activity; and Thomas drew upon the material in these four manuscript exercise notebooks throughout the thirties. He wrote to Henry Treece in July 1938: 'I have a great deal of material still, in MSS books, to shape into proper poems,'[36] suggesting that Thomas came to think of these Notebook poems as first drafts; and the manuscript versions of such poems as *The Hunchback in the Park* and *After the Funeral* indicate this. These notebooks are simply student exercise books. Astonishingly, they contain manuscript versions of just over half the poems eventually included in *18 Poems, Twenty-five Poems,* and *The Map of Love.* On reading the first notebooks one enters the peculiar, distinctive world of the early poetry, and they certainly confirm one's impression of the unity of composition in the early work. It is dangerous, however, to make generalizations from these manuscripts about Thomas's development, because while in a poem such as *Out of the Sighs* the manuscript version closely resembles the final form the poem took, in others the early manuscript was hardly more than a source. The final poem is sometimes recognizable only by an occasional line or phrase. As in the case of Yeats's poetry, the manuscript versions are usually easier to understand and often read like rough, prose versions of the later poem.

Out of the Sighs is a good example of a poem where there was only slight revision for inclusion in *Twenty-five Poems,* as the manuscript versions dated 7 July 1932 and 1 July 1932 indicate. The poem is a remarkable achievement, for Thomas wrote it when he was seventeen, and one treasures its uniquely personal tone as it registers a controlled yet all-humbling darkness of spirit. The first poem published by Thomas in a literary magazine was *And Death Shall have no Dominion*, published in *The New English Weekly* 18 May 1933. Again it is interesting to compare the notebook version (April 1933) and the final version of the opening stanza: the first version is easier to understand, the final one poetically richer and more evocative. Readers will observe the effective use of the transferred word giving new poetic life to a conventional phrase, whereby the familiar 'man in the moon' and 'west wind' becomes 'man in the wind and the west moon'.

Dylan Thomas wrote at least twice as much poetry up to 1934 as in his remaining nineteen years, so clearly this Swansea period was an exceedingly fertile one – though he chose not to publish the greater part of this verse. But what is most significant is the picture we have of a poet so certain of his poetic identity that once it was established (and I think this realization occurred early in 1934 about the time of *A process in the weather of the heart*), he published all but three of the poems he wrote from this time, February 1934, with the exception of the light verse. And that new voice that spoke so strikingly and originally in *18 Poems* (1934) did not basically change though it showed a continued growth in lucidity and in coherence of thought and feeling.

How was it that Thomas within a year or two turned from competent school-magazine versifier into an original poet? With the benefit of hindsight and the guidance provided by the poet in his letters, we can see that the poet realized – intuitively but with total conviction – 'the strong stressing of the physical'[37] was the basis of his style. Sound and the *physical* impact of poetry provides the key to Thomas's use of language. This essential feature of his writing, whereby the physical quality of thought and feeling is recorded, remains its dominant characteristic. The verbal links are less intellectual, logical and syntactical, than rhythmically determined and built upon syllabic and alliterative structures. Meaning in his verse, to a greater extent than is usual in English poetry, is in terms of affective and sensory perception. Thomas emphasized, in a letter written in November 1933, that it is through the physical body that man apprehends the world around him:

All thoughts and actions emanate from the body. Therefore the description of a thought or action – however abstruse it may be – can be beaten home by bringing it onto a physical level. Every idea, intuitive or intellectual, can be imaged and translated in terms of the body, its flesh, skin, blood, sinews, veins, glands, organs, cells or senses.[38]

Stressing the manner in which man is rooted in the earth, an essentially physical being, Thomas asserts in the same letter that:

The body, its appearance, death, and disease, is a fact, sure as the fact of a tree. It has its roots in the same earth as the tree. The greatest description I know of our own 'earthiness' is to be found in John Donne's Devotions, where he describes man as earth of the earth, his body earth, his hair a wild shrub growing out of the land.

Consequently Thomas's concept of poetry, suggesting as it does the pre-eminence of physical and sensory perception, implies an organic link between man and the natural world. And in Thomas nature is always seen as an organic power. This, expressed in various ways, is a major theme in his verse. In January 1934, during the crucial period that saw the emergence of his unique poetic voice, he wrote that 'It is my aim as an artist . . . to prove beyond doubt to myself that the flesh that covers me is the flesh that covers the sun, that blood in my lungs is the blood that goes up and down in a tree.'[39] Three months previously, in October 1933, Thomas had written the notable poem *The force that through the green fuse drives the flower*. It appears in the third (August 1933) notebook, and was published on 29 October 1933 in the *Sunday Referee*. It is a striking example of Thomas's use of rhythm and image, that 'strong stressing of the physical', to evoke the organic link between man and the natural world. The opening stanza asserts that human and natural life is subject to the same creative and destructive forces. Characteristically, Thomas relates this perception to himself:

> The force that through the green fuse drives the flower
> Drives my green age; that blasts the roots of trees
> Is my destroyer.
> And I am dumb to tell the crooked rose
> My youth is bent by the same wintry fever.

We may note in passing how the word 'green' is used in the first and second lines with a different emphasis in meaning, causing the reader to re-identify the particular meaning of each use. Hence, in the first line the word refers both to the life-giving force in the flower and, of course, to the green colour of the stem; in the second it describes the youth and innocence of the poet.

The second and third stanzas continue the expression of the idea of the unity of man and nature rather than develop the concept itself. Their effectiveness lies in the careful construction of sound and physical image, the repeated compulsive rhythm and renewed *physical* impact of the words, words that are usually of one syllable and in everyday usage; but their very forcefulness here suggests the care and deliberation in their selection:

> The force that drives the water through the rocks
> Drives my red blood; that dries the mouthing streams
> Turns mine to wax.
> And I am dumb to mouth unto my veins
> How at the mountain spring the same mouth sucks.

In the light of Thomas's earlier insistence that it is through the physical body that man apprehends all forms of experience, re-iterated in the same letter:

> Through my small, bonebound island I have learnt all I know,
> experienced all, sensed all. All I write is inseparable from
> the island . . .[38]

it is not surprising that the relationship of his own body to the world of nature is a major preoccupation.

In a related way, Thomas suggests in *When all my five and country senses see* that visionary experience (including the poetic) is attained through the improvement of sensory perception – a viewpoint that strongly recalls Blake's 'If the doors of perception were cleansed everything would appear infinite.'[40] Undoubtedly Thomas's genius in these years of late adolescence lay in the certainty with which he sought and found his own, distinctive, utterly original poetic voice. I have suggested ways in which the manuscript verse in the notebooks can guide us in tracing the evolution of this striking style and vision. Remembering the 'crooked rose' in the poem just discussed, with its echo of Blake's 'O Rose, thou art sick!' perhaps in reading Thomas's poetry we are wise to remember another of his early (1933) statements of poetic ancestry: 'I am in the path of Blake, but so far behind him that only the wings of his heels are in sight'[41], a characteristically felicitous and incisive comment by Dylan Thomas, reminding us inevitably, since Thomas was then only nineteen, of his kinship with Keats as a letter writer as well as poet.

The period following the First World War saw the emergence of Welshmen writing in English, among them Dylan Thomas, who had little in common with English literary movements in the inter-war years. These notable intruders included Caradoc Evans, Dylan Thomas, Vernon Watkins, Alun Lewis, Gwyn Thomas, Glyn Jones, and Gwyn Jones. As well as the fact that they write about Wales, they

Plate 17. Dylan Thomas, aged 19.

share a quality of style – fierce enthusiasm, energy, and flexibility – that links and distinguishes them. They also share a Welsh inclination to eloquence, a gift for metaphor, and an aptitude for sensory communication. Interestingly, when Stephen Spender said in his review of Dylan Thomas's *Collected Poems*:

Dylan Thomas represents a romantic revolt against this classicist tendency which has crystallized around the theological views of Eliot and Auden. It is a revolt against more than this, against the Oxford, Cambridge and Harvard intellectualism of much modern poetry in the English language; against the King's English of London and the South, which has become a correct idiom capable of refinements of beauty, but incapable of harsh effects, coarse texture and violent colours.[42]

41

Thomas wrote: '. . . this is now the clearest, most considered and sympathetic, and in my opinion, truest review that I have ever seen of my writing.'[43]

Undoubtedly, Dylan Thomas's was an original and revolutionary approach to the language of poetry, with its emphasis on the auditory, sensuous and affective use of words, sustained by strong, instinctive rhythms. Those features of style that we have been observing in his earliest published poems owe little to traditions in English poetry in the thirties. Rather do they derive from his Welsh background with its living tradition of exuberance in language – though allied to strict formal control in poetry. Anglo-Welsh writing exhibits a craftsmanlike delight in the sound and sensuous quality of words; a rejection of the English addiction to meiosis in favour of a more vivid, emotional, dramatized response to experience – and particularly is this true of the South Wales temperament and character.

Of these eloquent and dragon-tongued intruders into English literature, Gwyn Jones has written that 'this was the last generation that paid for emergence with its fathers' sweat and bruises; bible-blest and chapel-haunted, wrestle hard as we can, we stand confessed the last, lost nonconformists of an Age'.[44] The picture of Thomas as a lost Nonconformist, wrestling with an inherited, albeit declining religion, is close to the truth of his poetry. As we shall see in this poetry, Dylan Thomas is the poet who speaks for the age immediately following the age of faith. The belief in Christianity is a diminishing one, but its ethos and its mythology still provide the coinage of language and thought. He is left with the fact of his own body and the physical fact of this world, in all their rich potential. If we say that Dylan Thomas follows the age of belief, we must add that he precedes the totally secular age. His poetry links, in many ways unites, the religious and the secular imagination. It is a major achievement, and the paradox is radiantly sustained:

> Heaven that never was
> Nor will be ever is always true.

But we anticipate the end of the journey. For the Dylan Thomas of these Swansea years was influenced by a culture and environment which he was also at the time in rebellion against. Dylan Thomas grew 'from dragon's tooth to druid in his own land';[45] but we must not forget his adolescent rebellion, particularly against the narrow Nonconformist ethos:

*Plate 18. Paraclete
Congregational Church.*

No Welsh writer can hunt his bread and butter in Wales unless he pulls his forelock to the *Western Mail*, Bethesdas on Sunday, and enters public-houses by the back door and reads Caradoc Evans only when alone, and by candlelight.[46]

Caradoc Evans, the notable satirist, whom Dylan visited in Aberystwyth, on one occasion had the distinction of having his books burned. Dylan writes that:

We made a tour of the pubs in the evening, drinking to the eternal damnation of the Almighty and the soon-to-be-hoped-for destruction of the Tin Bethels. The University students love Caradoc and pelt him with stones whenever he goes out.[47]

The lighter side of Thomas's intransigent nature is reflected in his humorous attempts to shock the Nonconformist taste, as in the opening of the story *Where Tawe flows*:

The hunchback in the park,
A solitary mister
Propped between trees and water,
Going daft for fifty seven years,
So getting dafter,
A cripple children call at,
Half - laughing, by no other name than mister,
They shout hey mister
Running when he has heard them clearly
Past lake and rockery
On out of sight.

Plate 19. 1932 manuscript version of 'The Hunchback in the Park'.

Young Mr Thomas was at that moment without employment, but it was understood that he would soon be leaving for London to make a career in Chelsea as a free-lance journalist: he was penniless, and hoped, in a vague way, to live on women.

Certainly Dylan Thomas's eyes were now turned to the life of the metropolis, and in November 1934 he moved to London. *18 Poems* was published on 18 December of that year. To establish his poetic reputation he felt it necessary to live in London, where he could make his name as a poet and meet influential people. But he has left us a vivid, humorous, not entirely fanciful picture of his public self in Swansea, the provincial Bohemian:

above medium height. Above medium height for Wales, I mean, he's five foot six and a half. Thick blubber lips; snub nose; curly mousebrown hair; one front tooth broken after playing a game called Cats and Dogs in the Mermaid, Mumbles; speaks rather fancy; truculent; plausible; a bit of a shower-off; plus-fours and no breakfast, you know . . . a bombastic adolescent provincial Bohemian with a thick-knotted artist's tie made out of his sister's scarf . . . a gabbing, ambitious, mock-tough, pretentious young man.[48]

The public figure was already established, for there was a strong the-atrical impulse in Thomas's personality. It was in something of this bohemian mood that he left Wales for London with the amusing, albeit self-deceiving comment: 'The land of my fathers. My fathers can keep it.'[49]

PART II

Exile and Return Journeys: 1934–1949

Though Dylan Thomas moved to London in November 1934 and did not settle permanently in Wales until he moved to the Boat House, Laugharne, in 1949, he was always returning during these intervening years. He often stayed with his parents in Swansea; he lived in Laugharne from the spring of 1938 until July 1940; and after this there were long stays with his parents in Bishopston, a village on the Gower. He also spent a year at New Quay, Cardiganshire.

Dylan Thomas's first address in London was 5 Redcliffe Street, sharing a room with his Swansea friend Fred Janes. Mervyn Levy lived in the same house, which was at the Earls Court end of Chelsea. Thomas has left a picture evocative both of their youthful sense of adventure and of their longing for Swansea:

in London, where we were exiled bohemian boily boys ... three very young monsters green and brimming from Swansea ... all living together in one big boring beautiful room ... in Redcliffe Gardens ... that's when the portrait of me, a frog in his salad days, was painted. But in those London days, I remember, we were terribly nostalgic too, about our town, Swansea.[1]

By December 1934 Dylan was already complaining of the 'most boring Bohemian parties' in this 'quarter of the pseudo-artists', finding it difficult to work in 'a room as muddled and messy as ours',[2] and talking of having met Henry Moore, Edwin Muir, and Wyndham Lewis. Dylan returned to Swansea for Christmas, and was back again in March, exhausted by the London life of drink, talk, parties – what he later called 'the capital punishment'. The pattern was set of return journeys to Wales, where he could best do his serious work – the writing of poems and stories rather than reviews and later film scripts – looked after first by his mother, then by his wife. In Wales he was less distracted by the temptations of casual drinking sessions and casual sex that London, in particular Soho, offered the young poet. His favourite drinking haunts were the French pub in Dean Street, Soho, the Fitzroy

Tavern close by, the old Café Royal and the Gargoyle Club; and drinking cronies at this time included Geoffrey Grigson, William Empson, Norman Cameron and Oswell Blakeston. Dylan had acquired his style for his London performances – and very good performances they were too; for undoubtedly he was an inspired raconteur, with an exhilarating verbal energy and comic inventiveness. He was never short of drinking companions despite his need to cadge his drinks! Dylan attended the Surrealist Exhibition in June 1936, offering boiled string in cups with the inquiry 'weak or strong?' His role as *enfant terrible* in Swansea was a more vivid and fruitful one. Certainly he remained critical of London literary life and its cosmopolitan culture, though he was ready from time to time to avail himself of its favours and pleasures. In a familiar lament to Vernon Watkins he criticizes London life because it lacks, he claims, a sense of good and evil. The Welsh puritan in Dylan Thomas retrospectively complains of 'three dark days in London, city of the restless dead . . . its intelligentsia is so hurried in the head that nothing stays there . . . there's no difference between good and evil'.[3]

Dylan Thomas's second collection, *Twenty-Five Poems*, was published in September 1936, and continues the rebellious self-questioning themes of *18 Poems*. The poet's main concerns are death, sex, sin, and the isolation of the individual. *Ears in the turrets hear* is perhaps the most clearly imaged and focused statement of his feelings of isolation and fear of contact (emotional? sexual?) with another:

> Ears in the turrets hear
> Hands grumble on the door,
> Eyes in the gables see
> The fingers at the locks.
> Shall I unbolt or stay
> Alone till the day I die
> Unseen by stranger-eyes
> In this white house?
> Hands, hold you poison or grapes?

It is a haunting stanza, where the firm short-lined rhythms nevertheless subtly hint and echo the young man's uncertainty ('grumble', 'fingers at the locks') and fears, locked like a maiden in his tower. The ambiguously linked 'poison' and 'grapes' is the very essence of puritan conflict and guilt, with its intimations of alcoholic indulgence ('what's your poison?'). The 'white house' suggests the body and the second stanza confirms this, echoing as it does the poet's account (in a letter written some three months after this poem) of the privacy of the 'bonebound island':

> Beyond this island bound
> By a thin sea of flesh
> And a bone coast,
> The land lies out of sound
> And the hills out of mind.
> No birds or flying fish
> Disturbs this island's rest.

'Through my small bonebound island I have learnt all I know, experienced all, and sensed all'[4] writes the poet. May ships, sailors visit? The metaphor is clearly, resonantly developed; desire for experience, for communication stirs like a flame in the wind:

> Ears in this island hear
> The wind pass like a fire,
> Eyes in this island see
> Ships anchor off the bay.
> Shall I run to the ships
> With the wind in my hair,
> Or stay till the day I die
> And welcome no sailor?
> Ships hold you poison or grapes?

With continuing clarity of direction, and masterly repetition and development of rhythm and image the poet focuses his dilemma as the poem comes to its close; earlier words ('grumble', 'stranger') brought back like remembered harmonies:

> Hands grumble on the door,
> Ships anchor off the bay,
> Rain beats the sand and slates.
> Shall I let in the stranger,
> Shall I welcome the sailor,
> Or stay till the day I die?

Orchestrated metaphor, thought, and feeling make their final chime, and a young man's uncertainty, fear and questioning, reverberate still in the mind:

> Hands of the stranger and holds of the ships,
> Hold you poison or grapes?

Thomas wrote this poem when he was nineteen, for there was very little change on publication in *Twenty-Five Poems*; though interestingly on first publication it was helpfully titled *Dare I?* Interestingly, too, its imagery of approaching ships, viewed from above the bay in a building where rain beats on sand and slates, brings to mind the view from

Dylan's room in Cwmdonkin Drive, gabled houses and windy streets running down to Swansea bay.

An illuminating comparison with this poem is provided by *Especially when the October wind*, again initially a poem of introspective stasis, for the poet begins with the experiencing world of his own body; but this is related outward to and set against the actual world of the poet's hillside Swansea home. While it is true that Thomas employs 'the scenery of the (bonebound) island to describe the scenery of my thoughts, the earthquake of the body to describe the earthquake of the heart',[4] nevertheless, what impinges on the bodily perceptions of the poet is a particular environment, a landscape of leafless trees ('winter sticks'), October sun and wind, and the nearby seashore and seabirds:

> Especially when the October wind
> With frosty fingers punishes my hair,
> Caught by the crabbing sun I walk on fire
> And cast a shadow crab upon the land,
> By the sea's side, hearing the noise of birds,
> Hearing the raven cough in winter sticks,
> My busy heart who shudders as she talks
> Sheds the syllabic blood and drains her words.

The second stanza closes in on Thomas's sense of isolation as a poet as he talks of his attempt to register experience in terms of verbal patterns. In his room he is 'shut in a tower of words', women are 'wordy shapes' as they walk in Cwmdonkin Park, the children innocently, limbs akimbo, at play – 'star-gestured' – (the adjective following the noun in Welsh fashion; c.f. 'heron priested shore', 'sea-wet church'). He would speak too with voice of beech and oak, as well as the sea's language:

> Shut, too, in a tower of words, I mark
> On the horizon walking like the trees
> The wordy shapes of women, and the rows
> Of the star-gestured children in the park.
> Some let me make you of the vowelled beeches,
> Some of the oaken voices, from the roots
> Of many a thorny shire tell your notes,
> Some let me make you of the water's speeches.

Stanza three considers man-made time ('the wagging clock' – the pendulum wagging back and forth, like a dog's tail) within the house; then the view from the window of the chiming church clock ('neural meaning' 'declaims') with its weather vane ('the windy weather in the cock'). The poet perceives a more significant concept of time – the seasons ('the meadow's signs'). It is the 'signal grass' that tells him of growth and decay of the processes of life and death – 'all flesh is grass' we may recall from our Bible reading:

> Behind a pot of ferns the wagging clock
> Tells me the hour's word; the neural meaning
> Flies on the shafted disk, declaims the morning
> And tells the windy weather in the cock.
> Some let me make you of the meadow's signs;
> The signal grass that tells me all I know
> Breaks with the wormy winter through the eye,
> Some let me tell you of the raven's sins.

The final stanza reminds us of the setting of the poem, of how Swansea rises in hill formations from the sea, rather like an amphitheatre, with the poet's home on the hillside high above the town – hence the reference to the 'loud hill of Wales', for it is loud with his words. The poem moves to its close as Thomas's inspiration passes, the 'poeticus furor' is gone, 'the scurry of chemic blood' eased – with its underlying sexual meaning. It is as though the sea itself has now become still, and only the birds call above the retreating waves:

> Especially when the October wind
> (Some let me make you of autumnal spells,
> The spider-tongued, and the loud hill of Wales)
> With fists of turnips punishes the land,
> Some let me make you of the heartless words.
> The heart is drained that spelling in the scurry
> Of chemic blood, warned of the coming fury.
> By the sea's side hear the dark-vowelled birds.

Two things were to turn Dylan's imagination outward, his marriage to Caitlin, and a few years later the impact of war. It was in April 1936 that Dylan met Caitlin Macnamara, in a pub called the Wheatsheaf in Soho, where they were introduced to each other by the celebrated Welsh painter and bohemian figure, Augustus John. Immediately, they became lovers, and were married in Penzance Registry Office in 1937. Dylan wrote with some excitement to Vernon Watkins from the Lobster Pot, a guest house in Mousehole, Cornwall, where he and Caitlin spent their honeymoon, that,

My own news is very big and simple. I was married three days ago to Caitlin Macnamara; in Penzance registry office; with no money, no prospect of money, no attendant friends or relatives, and in complete happiness.[5]

Plate 20. Dylan and Caitlin.

Shortly afterwards they moved to the home of Caitlin's mother in Blashford, Ringwood, Hampshire, where they lived in the months following their marriage.

In the summer of 1937 Keidrych Rhys published the first number of the literary magazine *Wales*. Dylan Thomas was a regular contributor, and is listed as co-editor of nos 6/7. Dylan's prose piece *Prologue to an Adventure* begins on the front cover of the first issue; while *Wales* Number 5 contained *Poem for Caitlin*, later titled from the first line *I make this in a warring absence*. It was in the spring of 1938 that Dylan and his wife first went to live in Laugharne, their first home a cottage in Gosport Street which Dylan described as 'a small, damp fisherman's furnished cottage' where 'the double-bed is a swing band'.[6] Inviting Henry Treece to stay that summer Thomas spoke of the 'garden leading down to mud and sea', the four poky rooms, and declared that 'you bathe or go dirty'. He commended 'three good pubs' and announced 'no prohibitive drinking hours' and the good talk therein with 'colossal liars to listen to'.[7] A month later, in late July 1938 he moved to 'Sea View', an altogether more comfortable, larger home and, says Dylan with characteristic humour, 'we've moved home and tilted our noses. Our previous house, once a palace, is now that cottage. Here we could have two bedrooms each, which is quite useless.'[8] But they were

Plate 21. The cottage in Gosport Street.

Plate 22. Sea View, Laugharne.

happy, albeit penniless, pre-war years. As well as his poetry Dylan was writing the stories of *Portrait of the Artist as a Young Dog*, that he called 'stories towards a provincial biography ... They are all about Swansea life: the pubs, clubs, billiard rooms, promenades, adolescence and the suburban nights, friendships, tempers and the humiliations.'[9] There were visits from Vernon Watkins, and visits to Vernon Watkins's home on Pennard Cliffs, Gower. It was the time of their closest friendship; and indeed shortly before moving to Laugharne Dylan had spent three months at his parents' home in Bishopston, only three miles from Vernon's home.

Though Dylan and Caitlin were very happy there were days when there was no money at all. In one letter Dylan writes of facing a weekend 'smokeless and breadless',[7] with only 'two poor dabs' (flat fish) in the kitchen, while his wife is 'out cockling' in the estuary. It was in January 1939, when Dylan and Caitlin were staying in Blashford, at the house of Caitlin's mother, that their first child Llewelyn was born, an event celebrated in the poems *A saint about to fall* and *If my head hurt a hair's foot*. In December Dylan had written to Vernon Watkins that 'we're just as poor ... but the ravens – soft, white, silly ravens – will feed us'.[10]

53

Plate 23. Croquet at Vernon Watkins's.

In the *Portrait* stories Thomas's view of Wales is a genial, and in so far as it is childhood and adolescence nostalgically recollected, a somewhat idealized one. Pathos and comedy are effectively combined, but it is the artist in comedy, with his eye turned sharply outward upon the world around him, who dominates. An earlier story *The Burning Baby* provides an interesting contrast. First published in 1936, it represents the poet's earlier, more introspective, obsessively sexual and darker vein of prose writing. It is closer to the primitive passions that are the world of Caradoc Evans's satiric tales. I am indebted to Glyn Jones's account of how, on a visit to Aberystwyth to meet Caradoc Evans, he told Dylan Thomas the story of Dr Price of Llantrisant. The doctor, who died in 1893 at the age of ninety-three, defied in a most exhibitionist fashion the legal, religious, and moral conventions of his time. He called himself a druid, and on his public appearances dressed in weird and highly-coloured costumes. He chanted pagan addresses to the moon and boasted of supernatural powers. His much-loved illegitimate son, whom he named Iesu Grist (Jesus Christ), died at the age of five months. Price carried him to the top of a hill in Caerlan fields and, chanting laments over the body, burned it. Dr Price was brought to court, and his acquittal led to the legalization of cremation in Great Britain.

Thomas listened to this story lounging on his bed at their Aberystwyth hotel and by the end, Glyn Jones recalls, the bed-sheet was riddled with cigarette burns, so total was Dylan's absorption in the story. Clearly Thomas's mind seized upon the incident of the child's cremation for *The Burning Baby* opens with a powerful focusing of fact and fantasy:

They said that Rhys was burning his baby when a gorse bush broke into fire on the summit of the hill. The bush, burning merrily, assumed to them the sad white features and the rickety limbs of the vicar's burning baby. What the wind had not blown away of the baby's ashes, Rhys Rhys had sealed in a stone jar.

After this vigorous, dramatic opening, the narrative continues:

It was, they said, on a fine sabbath morning in the middle of summer that Rhys Rhys fell in love with his daughter.

We learn, too, that the vicar's elder son, a changeling, an idiot, with long green hair, had enjoyed strange sexual adventures, for his sister 'was to him as ugly as the sowfaced woman of Llareggub who had taught him the terrors of the flesh. He remembered the advances of that unlovely woman!' Rhys's daughter conceives a child by him, and it is this child he burns:

Surrounded by shadows, he prayed before the flaming stack, and the sparks of the heather blew past him. Burn, child, poor flesh, mean flesh, flesh, flesh, sick sorry flesh, flesh of the foul womb, burn back to dust, he prayed.

Thomas makes a minister of religion the central character in the story, for the instinct to wound the Nonconformist clergy was as deeply rooted in young Dylan Thomas as it had been in Caradoc Evans. To attribute perverse desires to the religious and respectable is a simple but effective method of attack Thomas readily exploits, here with sardonic humour:

Rhys Rhys sat in his study, the stem of his pipe stuck between his flybuttons, the Bible unopened upon his knees. The day of God was over, and the sun, like another sabbath, went down behind the hills . . . Merry with desire, Rhys Rhys cast the Bible on the floor.

In this story the name Llareggub makes an early appearance, its spelling here more suggestive of its etymology (reversed, it reads 'bugger all') than the more familiar Llaregyb! How different, too, the amusing and disarming eccentricities of the preacher in *Under Milk Wood* who 'dips his pen in Cocoa' and hearing Polly Garter's song of sexual reminiscence innocently declares 'Praise the Lord! We are a musical nation!' It is a measure of Thomas's growth from 'dragon's tooth' to 'Druid in his own land'[11] that the phantasmagoria world of Wales of these early stories becomes, by way of the *Portrait*, broadcast tales and talks, *Under Milk Wood*'s 'White book of Llareggub' wherein we read of 'the innocence of men' in 'this place of love'. The wayward 'Nogood Boyo' may owe something to the idiot with green hair, and Bessie Bighead to the 'sowfaced woman of Llareggub' – albeit changed and transformed by Thomas's mature, compassionate imagination.

How different in style, background, and tone is the story *A Visit to Grandpa's*, probably the first of the autobiographical tales *Portrait of the Artist as a Young Dog*, written in these years immediately preceding the war. Here the rural life of West Wales is imaginatively and realistically evoked, and presented with that blend of humour and pathos that is the hallmark of Thomas's most successful prose. A strong sense of community, as well as the reactions of an enthralled, observing child, is dramatically portrayed. The scene that closes *A Visit to Grandpa's* is one of the most delightful, moving, and hauntingly memorable that Thomas wrote. It describes a situation that could only be found in Wales, where by tradition, much emphasis and concern is given to a person's place of burial. The elderly are usually anxious to be buried in their ancestral churchyard, a feeling which, in its philosophical acceptance of death, would attract Thomas's interest. The Grandfather in this tale disappears one morning. It is soon realized that he has gone to Llangadock – for he has put on his best waistcoat – to be buried. He is discovered, *en route*, in Carmarthen. The final scene has a delicate blend of comedy and high seriousness, and shows Thomas's gift for dramatic dialogue. It is street theatre that Welsh village and valley life unselfconsciously affords:

Mr Griff pointed his coloured stick at him.
'And what do you think you are doing on Carmarthen Bridge in the middle of the afternoon,' he said sternly, 'with your best waistcoat and your old hat?'
Grandpa did not answer, but inclined his face to the river wind, so that his beard was set dancing and wagging as though he talked, and watched the coracle men move, like turtles, on the shore.
Mr Griff raised his stunted barber's pole. 'And where do you think you are going,' he said, 'with your old black bog?'
Grandpa said: 'I am going to Llangadock to be buried,' and he watched the

coracle shells slip into the water lightly, and the gulls complain over the fish-filled water as bitterly as Mr Price complained:

'But you aren't dead yet, Dai Thomas.'

For a moment Grandpa reflected, then: 'There's no sense in lying dead in Llanstephan,' he said. 'The ground is comfy in Llangadock; you can twitch your legs without putting them in the sea.'

His neighbours moved close to him. They said:

'You aren't dead, Mr Thomas.'

'How can you be buried then?'

'Nobody's going to bury you in Llanstephan.'

'Come on home, Mr Thomas.'

'There's strong beer for tea.'

'And cake.'

But Grandpa stood firmly on the bridge, and clutched his bag to his side, and stared at the flowing river and the sky, like a prophet who has no doubt.

Thomas's grandfather, it seems, was reluctant to be buried in Llanstephan and wanted to be laid to rest in his old home, Llangadog, where 'the ground is comfy'. The closing comparison of the old man to 'a prophet who has no doubt', with its Biblical and druidic associations, is particularly effective.

In August 1939 *The Map of Love*, a collection of poems and stories, was published, followed by the autobiographical *Portrait of the Artist as a Young Dog* in 1940. Rejected for military service for health reasons – he was graded C3 – Dylan Thomas worked on documentary films during the war, living for a time in Chelsea. Under the impact of war Thomas's poetic vision both deepened and achieved a tragic resonance. It deepened in such joyous, lucid, and rhapsodic recollections of childhood as *Poem in October*; for he was driven to create sources of remembered happiness and luminous, identifiable worlds as touchstones of sanity and hope during years of destruction and countless human sufferings. And as our first great civilian war poet he brought a tragic resonance and a compelling ritual to such war poems as *Ceremony After a Fire Raid* and *A Refusal to Mourn the Death, by Fire, of a Child in London*. The 1939–45 war saw the first deliberate and massive bombing of civilian populations, so that the incendiary raids on London in 1940 kept, with a savage irony, the home fires burning. Characteristically Thomas's most famous war poem *A Refusal to Mourn the Death, by Fire, of a Child in London*, though inspired by present horror, seeks an ancient lineage in its response to the scene and event of death by bombing. Importantly, Thomas's emotional concern is now turned outward to the sufferings of other people. Paradoxically, though he refuses to mourn he does write an elegy for the dead child. He refuses to mourn

Plate 24. Dylan and Caitlin in Chelsea.

because the fact of death must be accepted. Never until the end of the world, will he mourn. It is an ending imaged in terms of the Biblical account of its first creation, whereby that unifying darkness in which human, animal and vegetable life is fathered ('Bird beast and flower/ Fathering') obliterates light, sound, and the sea's life:

> Never until the mankind making
> Bird beast and flower

> Fathering and all humbling darkness
> Tells with silence the last light breaking
> And the still hour
> Is come of the sea tumbling in harness

And never until his own death, whereby he returns to the primal elements of earth and water (here given a symbolic identity as 'Zion of the water bead', 'synagogue of the ear of corn'):

> And I must enter again the round
> Zion of the water bead
> And the synagogue of the ear of corn

will the poet by prayer or tears lament the burning of the child (we may note echoes of 'the valley of the shadow of death'):

> Shall I let pray the shadow of a sound
> Or sow my salt seed
> In the least valley of sackcloth to mourn
> The majesty and burning of the child's death.

We learn that the poet refuses on the grounds of the pointlessness of mourning and protest because the child has now rejoined the elements from which she came: her body has become part of the earth's (not human) existence. The brief differentiated identity of human life has returned to a more familiar, ancient, elemental unity ('robed in the long friends'). In this literal and mystical reunion with mother earth and the veins of the mother from whom she was born, the child's existence is not subject to mortality ('the grains beyond age'). The water of the riding Thames is unmourning for it is part of the process of life and death (transformation that London's daughter has suffered):

> Deep with the first dead lies London's daughter,
> Robed in the long friends,
> The grains beyond age, the dark veins of her mother,
> Secret by the unmourning water
> Of the riding Thames.
> After the first death, there is no other.

There is of course the ambiguity of the final line. Is it a belief in Christian immortality or a simpler belief in the return to first elements (the more commonly held idea of 'pushing up the daisies')? Rather, it is a riveting instance of Dylan Thomas's poetry as the bridge between the religious and secular imagination. We are left with the fact of our own bodies and this physical world, but have retained a language and mythology that haunts and enriches our imaginative life. Consequently this elegy for the victim of an incendiary raid in 1940 employs language whose imaginative resources have roots in the Christian and Pre-Christian beliefs; here translated into terms both ancient and modern. The oratorical opening of the poem reminds us that Thomas is indeed a preacher in verse, for the absence of punctuation at the end of each line in the first two stanzas instructs us in the ritualistic structure of the poem. As in a chant, the voice must retain a high pitch at each line-ending until the full stop of the thirteenth line. This is how Dylan Thomas reads the poem.

It is illuminating to set beside this last stanza of *A Refusal to Mourn*, Wordsworth's very similar lines in *A Slumber did my Spirit Seal:*

> No motion has she now, no force;
> She neither hears nor sees,
> Rolled round in earth's diurnal course
> With rocks and stones and trees!

The difference is at once apparent: Wordsworth states simply and meditatively the familiar idea both poets celebrate; it is also Shelley's 'He is made one with nature'.[12] What the power of image and rhetoric contributes to Thomas's lines, in addition to the enriching ambiguities, is a *sense* of the motion, the force, the child now shares in the elemental unity she has joined. Meaning in Dylan Thomas's poem is as much the physical and sensory enactment of the idea as its linguistic statement. Similarly, when Thomas spoke in the opening stanza of the very seas being stilled, the power and originality of the poetry reside in the sense of the physical energy of the sea the lines evoke: 'tumbling' of course suggests primal sexual energy, and 'harness' is a small but richly significant shift in the more familiar image of the 'white horses' to describe tempestuous but controlled sea-waves. It is this combination of a compulsive rhythm and an emotionally, sensuously evocative, yet intellectually exact, image, that is the hallmark of Thomas's poetry at its most successful.

In prose, too, the impact of civilian suffering in war deepened Thomas's vision, as in his evocation of bombed Swansea in *Return Journey*. It is a search for a lost self, as, walking through Swansea, the poet looks 'for someone after fourteen years'. The script has a dramatic structure, based on the narrator's questioning of several distinct groups – the pub clientele, reporters, passers-by, teachers. No doubt Thomas's war time work in documentary films had developed his ability to create dramatizations of places and people. The opening picture of war-damaged Swansea High Street in winter snow, the only movement that of wandering dogs and romping boys, is essentially an elegy of loss:

It was a cold white day in High Street, and nothing to stop the wind slicing up from the docks, for where the squat and tall shops had shielded the town from the sea lay their blitzed flat graves marbled with snow and headstoned with fences. Dogs, delicate as cats on water, as though they had gloves on their paws, padded over the vanished buildings.

Swansea had suffered three days' bombing, a cutting off of the past as irremediable but so much more brutal than time's passing; and once familiar places are level, chill, white desert where children play:

Boys romped, calling high and clear, on top of a levelled chemist's and a shoe shop, and a little girl, wearing a man's cap, threw a snowball in a chill deserted garden that had once been the Jug and Bottle of the Prince of Wales.

Sometimes the elegy for wartime destruction is presented humorously, the sense of loss no less poignant. 'What's the Three Lamps like now?' asks the poet of the pub he frequented as a young Swansea journalist. 'It isn't like anything. It isn't there. It's nothing mun. You remember Ben Evans's stores? It's right next door to that. Ben Evans isn't there either,' replies a fellow-drinker. 'The flat white wastes where all the shops had been' are background to the surviving humour and humanity of the Swansea people the poet meets. 'I remember a man came here with a monkey,' reminisces the hotel barmaid. 'Called for 'alf for himself and a pint for the monkey. And he wasn't Italian at

Plate 25. Majoda.

all. Spoke Welsh like a preacher.' But mostly it is the voices of the past we hear, and hear in memory and in memoriam:

The voices of fourteen years ago hung silent in the snow and ruin, and in the falling winter morning I walked on through the white havoc'd centre.

An important return journey Thomas made in the late summer of 1944 was to New Quay, Cardiganshire, where he lived for a year in a wood and asbestos bungalow called 'Majoda', a rather isolated house half a mile or so from the town. Unlike that other village by the sea, Laugharne, New Quay was a cliffside village descending by a precipitous hill to the busy harbour. Dylan's pub here was the Black Lion, and his amusing poem *New Quay* evokes the scene and the seaside village atmosphere:

> The darkening sea flings Lea
> And Perrins on the cockled tablecloth
> Of mud and sand. And, like a sable moth,
> A cloud against the glassy sun flutters his
> Wings . . . .
>   Sinister dark over Cardigan
> Bay. No-good is abroad. I unhardy can
> Hardly bear the din of No-good wracked dry on
> The pebbles. It is time for the Black Lion
> But there is only Buckley's unfrisky
> Mild. Turned again, Worthington. Never whisky.[13]

Plate 26. The Black Lion, New Quay.

Plate 27. New Quay harbour.

Undoubtedly this writing anticipates both the comedy and gentler satire of *Under Milk Wood*. Even more does the broadcast talk *Quite Early One Morning*, in which the poet walks through a small Welsh town by the sea and describes the inhabitants and their dreams. This was written in New Quay, and read by Dylan Thomas on the B.B.C. Welsh Home Service in August 1945. In early morning, following a tempestuous night, the sea is calm, 'the quay shouldering out, nobody on it now but the gulls and the capstans;' and looking at the seascape below, the poet sees 'the splashed church, with a cloud in the shape of a bell poised above it, ready to drift and ring' for it is also a 'sea-wet church'. We have, too, a sense of the precipitous 'cliff-perched town' aptly and vividly evoked, its 'salt-white houses dangling over water', its 'bow-windowed villas squatting prim in neatly treed but unsteady hill streets'. Though there are many echoes of *Under Milk Wood*, the characters are introduced through the poet-narrator rather than dramatically presented. But the comedy in their presentation touches the same notes of fantasy and chapel-baiting humour:

In the head of Miss Hughes, 'The Cosy', clashed the cymbals of an eastern court. Eunuchs struck gongs the size of Bethesda Chapel. Sultans with voices fiercer than visiting preachers demanded a most un-Welsh dance.

Indeed the chapel still symbolizes a stern, unloving, unjoyous Nonconformist ethos, and it is playfully mocked:

Plate 28. View of New Quay from Majoda.

The Chapel stood grim and grey, telling the day there was to be no nonsense. The chapel was not asleep, it never cat-napped nor nodded nor closed its long cold eye. I left it telling the morning off and the sea-gull hung rebuked above it.

The characters, as voices heard in the early morning, are presented in verse. In interesting contrast to the genial, innocent and certain faith of *Under Milk Wood*'s Reverend Eli Jenkins, an affectionate portrait of a Nonconformist preacher, Thomas's picture here is of a Minister worried by doubt:

> Parchedig Thomas Evans making morning tea,
> Very weak tea, too, you mustn't waste a leaf.
> Every morning making tea in my house by the sea,
> I am troubled by one thing only, and that belief.

On a familiar note of joy and pathos Thomas ends this short piece; his ability in prose to strike many notes by deft, richly inventive, and imaginative use of language is moving towards dramatic composition:

Thus some of the voices of a cliff-perched town at the far end of Wales moved out of sleep and darkness into the new-born, ancient, and ageless morning, moved and were lost.

Clearly this place, and the characters described here, provided the seed of *Under Milk Wood* that was to flower in the village and sea-scapes of

Plate 29. Gelli, Talsarn.

Laugharne. Thomas has registered here, too, not only his gift for comedy but that intuition of a timeless innocence and joy that gives unique radiance to his view of the human condition.

A second child, Aeronwy Thomas, was born in 1943. In the summer of 1942, Caitlin had lived in Talsarn, a Cardiganshire village in the beautiful valley of the river Aeron, a name later remembered and given to the child. While on a visit from war-time London, Dylan wrote, 'I have been here for over a week with Caitlin, with milk and mild and cheese and eggs, and I feel fit as a fiddle ... I watch the sun from a cool room.'[14] 1946 saw the publication of *Deaths and Entrances*, and during this time Thomas was doing a great deal of writing and performing for the B.B.C. From March 1946 until May 1949 he lived near Oxford, visiting Italy in the spring of 1947 and Prague in March 1949. In his return journeys to Wales Thomas's poetic inspiration increasingly centred on that re-creation of remembered childhood landscapes, places that keep something of what he called 'our Edenie hearts'.[15] 'It's a poem about happiness,'[15] said Dylan in 1950 about the projected poem *In Country Heaven*. The first, and perhaps most famous of his poems 'about happiness' was *Fern Hill*, named after the Carmarthenshire farm whose landscapes and 'remembered tellings'[15] it is now time to visit.

PART III

Fern Hill and Childhood

'The Country is holy: O bide in that country kind.'[1]

The Carmarthenshire countryside of Fern Hill, Llangain, and Llan-stephan becomes the setting of the nostalgic re-creations of childhood, as in *Fern Hill* and such autobiographical stories as *A Visit to Grandpa's* and *The Peaches*. These other return journeys to the visionary and de-lightful country of childhood are deeply rooted in the lives and land-scapes of this corner of West Wales that Dylan had known from his earliest days. However, the note of mortality rings through both the comic prose and the poetry of ecstatic recollection, its pathos deepening Thomas's vision of childhood's – as of life's – transient joy.

Fern Hill, called 'Gorsehill' in his story *The Peaches*, stood on a rise that sloped down to a stream and wooded valley or dingle. The farm-house was surrounded by tall fir trees, and the farm and its buildings formed three sides of a court. An orchard completed the setting that was to be so radiantly transformed into that world of child, animals, trees, grass and sunlight. When it was kept as a small holding by Annie and Jim Jones in the 1920s, its few cows, pigs and chickens enabled them to scrape a living. It seems Annie did most of the work, her husband being fond of his drink – as the opening of *The Peaches* sug-gests; for he leaves young Dylan waiting in the cart while drinking with the proceeds from a piglet he sells. Finally *en route* in the cart Uncle Jim 'sang hymns all the way to Gorsehill in an affectionate bass voice, and conducted the wind with his whip'. We learn from his son Gwilym, who is studying for the Ministry, that 'Last Christmas he took a sheep over his shoulder, and he was pissed for ten days.' Arriving at the farm young Dylan revels in the light and warmth of the welcome: 'I saw the plates on the shelves, the lighted lamp on the long, oil-clothed table, "Prepare to Meet Thy God" knitted over the fire place, the smil-ing china dogs, the brown-stained settle, the grandmother clock, and ran into the kitchen and into Annie's arms.' It was a country life whose earthiness was very different from suburban Swansea.

Plate 30. Dylan and his mother at 'Fern Hill'.

Significantly, it was the poem that commemorates Annie's death, *After the funeral*, which first turned Thomas's imagination outward from his own introspective concerns and focused it on the life of another person. *After the funeral*, written in 1938, represents the beginning of his poetic maturity. With perception and apt critical insight Thomas commented in a B.B.C. reading of the poem in 1949 that it 'is the only one I have written that is, directly, about the life and death of one particular human being I knew – and not about the very many lives and deaths whether seen, as in my first poems, in the tumultuous world of my own being or, as in the later poems, in war, grief, and the great holes and corners of universal love.'[2] It was no doubt his self-regarding adolescence, and its self dramatization, that explains the poet's callous response to Ann's death in 1933. In a letter he writes of his feelings on getting the news that his aunt Ann Jones is dying of cancer, the 'insanitary farm' is of course *Fern Hill*:

'As I am writing, a telegram arrives. Mother's sister, who is in the Carmarthen Infirmary suffering from cancer of the womb, is dying. After Mother's departure I am left alone in the house, feeling slightly theatrical. Telegrams, dying aunts, cancer, especially of such a private part as the womb, distraught mother and unpremeditated train journeys come rarely. Many summer weeks I spent happily with the cancered aunt on her insanitary farm. She loved me quite inordinately, gave me sweets and money, though she could ill afford it, petted, patted, and spoiled me. She writes – is it, I wonder a past tense yet – regularly. Her postscripts are endearing. She still loves – or loved – me, though I don't know why . . .

But the foul thing is I feel utterly unmoved . . . I shall miss her bi-annual postal orders. And yet I like – liked her. She loves – loved me. Am I . . . callous and hasty? Should I weep? Should I pity the old thing? For a moment I feel I should. There must be something lacking in me.'[3]

Ann Jones died on 7 February 1933, and the February 1933 Notebook contains the manuscript poem written on 10 February, presumably the day of the funeral. Its opening lines, in particular the first two, are closely echoed in the final poem, registering a satiric view of the mourners, with their vain chatter, mulish praise of the deceased:

> After the funeral mule praises, brays,
> Shaking of mule heads, betoken
> Grief at the going to earth of man
> Or woman, at yet another long woe broken.[4]

The dead woman is referred to in rather general terms and, as in the letter, with little sense of personal loss or grief:

> At (he or she), loved or else hated well,
> So far from love or hate (,) in a deep hole.

It is the assumed hypocritical tears and prayers of the mourners that rouse the poet rather than protest at this death:

> The mourners in their Sabbath black
> Drop tears unheeded or choke back a sob
> Join in the hymns, and mark with dry bright looks
> The other heads, (bent), spying, on black books.

These lines by a rebellious nineteen year old are directed more at the conventional religion of the mourners; nevertheless they are the source of the anger and protest of the man who five years later composed an elegy of deeply felt and passionate concern:

> After the funeral, mule praises, brays
> Windshake of sailshaped ears, muffle-toed tap
> Tap heavily of one peg in the thick
> Grave's foot, blinds down the lids, the teeth in black,
> The spittled eyes, the salt ponds in the sleeves.

He is still embittered by the facile and – to him – inadequate acquiescence of the bereaved, who find sufficient comfort in their conventions of belief and burial; but the final poem focuses magnificently on the life and virtues of Ann, whom Thomas called 'an ancient peasant aunt'[5] in his letter to Vernon Watkins enclosing the completed poem. Significantly, the circumstances of the funeral initially awaken in Thomas the reactions of the boy to whom Ann and 'Fern Hill' meant so much:

> Morning smack of the spade that wakes up sleep,
> Shakes a desolate boy who slits his throat
> In the dark of the coffin and sheds dry leaves.

I recall Vernon Watkins telling me that Thomas, when writing this poem, was anxious to take his images from common, everyday, domestic things and not to move from the humble origins and familiar simplicities of his aunt's home and life. Now, after the funeral meats and funeral griefs, it is the adult poet who is in the parlour from which the body has just been taken, the familiar Welsh parlour used only for funerals and on Sundays, dusty and full of ornaments:

> After the feast of tear-stuffed time and thistles
> In a room with a stuffed fox and a stale fern,
> I stand, for this memorial's sake, alone
> In the snivelling hours with dead, humped Ann

It is the parlour described in his story *The Peaches*, with the stuffed fox, the fern, a Bible, a room and a place that was always to haunt Thomas's imagination:

The best room smelt of moth-balls and fur and damp and dead plants and stale, sour air. Two glass cases on wooden coffin-boxes lined the window wall. You looked at the weed-grown vegetable garden through a stuffed fox's legs, over a partridge's head, along the red-paint-stained breast of a stiff, wild duck. A case of china and pewter, trinkets, teeth, family brooches, stood beyond the bandy table; there was a large oil lamp on the patchwork tablecloth, a Bible with a clasp, a tall vase with a draped woman about to bathe on it, and a framed photograph of Annie, Uncle Jim, and Gwilym smiling in front of a fern-pot . . . The fireplace was full of brass tongs, shovels, and pokers. The best room was rarely used. Annie dusted and brushed and polished there once a week . . .

Ann's heart is described as 'fountain', and 'hooded' suggests the self-lessness of her love with its echoes of the hood of a nun, for it re-freshed those 'parched worlds of Wales'; nevertheless the poet knows she would have been too humble to accept such praise (to her 'a monstrous image') though 'puddles' brings us back to the homelier farm yard:

> Whose hooded, fountain heart once fell in puddles
> Round the parched worlds of Wales and drowned each sun
> (Though this for her is a monstrous image blindly
> Magnified out of praise; her death was a still drop;
> She would not have me sinking in the holy
> Flood of her heart's fame; she would lie dumb and deep
> And need no druid of her broken body).

But the 'flood' of her love is holy and as bard and druid – words with echoes of the ancient Welsh poet, prophet, and priest – Thomas insists on building this mythology of her love. Her virtue is meek and does not speak of itself (wood-tongued), but standing on the hearth of her poor, shabby home the poet calls on the seas and their buoys' bells to celebrate her love, so that the natural world of trees ('brown chapel') and birds, the 'ferned and foxy woods', sing her praise above the 'hymning heads' of the mourners. It is a service of nature, not the chapel, the myth-making poet creates:

> But I, Ann's bard on a raised hearth, call all
> The seas to service that her wood-tongued virtue
> Babble like a bellbuoy over the hymning heads,
> Bow down the walls of the ferned and foxy woods
> That her love sing and swing through a brown chapel,
> Bless her bent spirit with four, crossing birds.

The poet emphasizes the humility of the dead woman, the menial surroundings, the atrophied religion, in this panegyric. The cadence seems finally to enact a transfiguration, and her suffering and physical decay are replaced by marmoreal serenity:

> Her flesh was meek as milk, but this skyward statue
> With the wild breast and blessed and giant skull
> Is carved from her in a room with a wet window
> In a fiercely mourning house in a crooked year.
> I know her scrubbed and sour humble hands
> Lie with religion in their cramp, her threadbare
> Whisper in a damp word, her wits drilled hollow,
> Her fist of a face died clenched on a round pain;
> And sculptured Ann is seventy years of stone.

The closing lines continue the transformation, and the parlour's fox and fern become symbols of eternity. Conventional attitudes to death and religion are dismissed in favour of the natural immortality ensured by the biological processes of returning life ('the fern lay seeds'), and a belief in love as the supreme spiritual force vindicated even by the

Plate 31.
Annie Jones's
Grave.

hunted fox. Shakespeare's 'cloud-topped' is echoed in the satiric 'cloud sopped', which mocks the conventional belief in heaven – a sop. The poem is mythopoeic ('monumental argument'), for it creates a monument, elegy and myth for and of Ann's love, and also a 'hewn' artefact, for stone-like it is carved only with great effort, artistry, and skill.

Primarily, however, we are left with the stark image of the gravestone with its carved words of faith and commemoration, and the funeral rites of hymns and psalms, the grim panoply of the act of burial. These very real things shall storm over and trouble me, declares the poet; for as they are real to him, so the religion they represent was real to Ann:

> These cloud-sopped, marble hands, this monumental
> Argument of the hewn voice, gesture and psalm,
> Storm me forever over her grave until
> The stuffed lung of the fox twitch and cry Love
> And the strutting fern lay seeds on the black sill.

Dylan Thomas is mindful that, whatever its limitations, this Nonconformist faith produced a person of remarkable love and virtue in his aunt Ann Jones. It is the word 'virtue' that in addition to the fox and fern rings through the poem; not a commonly used word nowadays in this older, traditional sense with its echoes of a Roman heroic ideal combining goodness and strength.

As we have seen, it was a return to the early Notebooks that provided the source of this poem, though virtually a new composition emerged from the poet's working on the early draft. We have seen too how concern for another person deepened and strengthened Thomas's inspiration, giving it imaginative expanse and outer direction as well as inner compulsion. The impact of war extended this growth and its horrors contributed to the poet's impulse to re-create childhood's lost vision – as in *Fern Hill*. However, I think a third important factor in the emergence of his mature and finest verse was a very practical one, closely connected with his early sources of inspiration. In 1941 Thomas sold the early Notebooks, a bold and brave act which marked a decisive break with his poetry of adolescence. It was a break of which Thomas, again his own best critic, was vividly aware. 'It's lovely when you burn your boats,' he declared. 'They burn so beautifully.'[6]

Dylan was then twenty-six, the age at which Keats died, and those notebooks he was parting with were the tangible links with his youth, with Dylan the young poet. No longer was there the inspiration or example to return to his introspective world. It proved a decisive, and rewarding conflagration. Now childhood joys had to be re-created, the vision made again.

In some rough notes jotted down towards the end of his life Thomas spoke of Fern Hill as 'a place with which I have come to associate all the summer of my chil(dhood) . . . a lovely farm – a lonely farm – and a place with which I have come to associate all the golden – never shone a sun like that old rolling . . .'[7] In *Fern Hill* it is of course the same farm, the same settings as in the 'fiercely mourning' locations of *After the funeral* but now it is the gold coinage of childhood that illuminates orchard and farmyard, live fox and lilting house. Thomas re-creates in a physical and direct way the experience of childhood, and one recalls Vernon Watkins's revealing comment that 'out of a lump of texture or nest of phrases he created music, testing everything by physical feeling'.[8] The ecstatic state of joy and wonder is produced by an irresistible rhythmic spell and an emotive and sensuous use of word and image stunningly sustained:

> Now as I was young and easy under the apple boughs
> About the lilting house and happy as the grass was green,
>   The night above the dingle starry,

Plate 32. Trees behind 'Fern Hill'.

> Time let me hail and climb
> Golden in the heydays of his eyes,
> And honoured among wagons I was prince of the apple towns
> And once below a time I lordly had the trees and leaves
> Trail with daisies and barley
> Down the rivers of the windfall light.

As a boy on Ann Jones's farm the poet was a 'prince', 'lordly' in his happiness and freedom. Time was then kind to him, for he was unaware of mortality, innocent, and ignorant of mutability and death. Thomas's childhood tale begins not once upon but 'once below a time'. Scenes flow by in a visionary flux: 'apple boughs' . . . 'apple towns' . . . 'windfall light', and the visionary experience is there to be shared if we are emotionally and sensuously alive enough to register the impact:

> And as I was green and carefree, famous among the barns
> About the happy yard and singing as the farm was home,
> In the sun that is young once only,
> Time let me play and be
> Golden in the mercy of his means,
> And green and golden I was huntsman and herdsman, the calves
> Sang to my horn, the foxes on the hills barked clear and cold,
> And the sabbath rang slowly
> In the pebbles of the holy streams.

The sun is young once only since it is only once seen with eyes of childhood, and how different this from the image of the 'meat-eating sun', 'the crabbing sun', that haunts the early poems! In the third stanza, with its opening echo of the familiar 'all the day long' changed to the radiantly flowing 'all the sun long', the boy's excitement discovers a landscape of fiery vision ('fire green as grass'), the chimney smoke as music ('the tunes from the chimneys'), house-high hayfields and the ubiquitous stream in one sensory flux, recalling Rimbaud's '*Le Poëte se fait voyant par un long, immense et raisonné dérèglement de tous les sens*'. This reasoned derangement of the senses peculiar to the visionary poet reminds us that Dylan once called himself 'The Rimbaud of Cwmdonkin Drive'[9]. Night, too, enjoys this visionary flux as owls bear away the farm, night-jars, ricks and horses moving into the moonlit dark, for 'all the night long' has become the mysteriously refulgent 'all the moon long':

> All the sun long it was running, it was lovely, the hay
> Fields high as the house, the tunes from the chimneys, it was air
> And playing, lovely and watery
> And fire green as grass.

> And nightly under the simple stars
> As I rode to sleep the owls were bearing the farm away,
> All the moon long I heard, blessed among stables, the night-jars
> Flying with the ricks, and the horses
> Flashing into the dark.

Ricks, horses, stable, daisies and barley, cockerel and barn are of course a familiar part of the farm scene. Thomas's recording of his impressions as he falls asleep is close to his description of the visit to the farm in *The Peaches*:

The candle flame jumped in my bedroom window where a lamp was burning very low, and the curtains waved; the water in a glass on a round table by the bed stirred, I thought, as the door closed ... There was a stream below the window; I thought it lapped against the house all night until I slept.

There is a quicker movement in the opening line of the next stanza as the child wakes to a new day and the farm returns in all its pristine innocence and glory, appearing to the boy as Eden did to Adam, all created life singing its morning praises. The farm is personified as a returning wanderer, with a sensuous richness akin to Keats's personification of autumn in its beauty and apt detail:

> And then to awake, and the farm, like a wanderer white
> With the dew, come back, the cock on his shoulder: it was all
> Shining, it was Adam and maiden,
> The sky gathered again
> And the sun grew round that very day.
> So it must have been after the birth of the simple light
> In the first, spinning place, the spellbound horses walking warm
> Out of the whinnying green stable
> On to the fields of praise.

This closely resembles Traherne's: 'I saw all in the peace of Eden; Heaven and Earth did sing my creator's praises, and could not make more melody to Adam than to me. All Time was Eternity and a perpetual Sabbath.'[10] So the farm landscapes and animals – for the child is the only person present – are re-created as the lost golden world, Eden before the Fall, when the young Dylan, like the seventeenth century mystical poet Henry Vaughan, 'shin'd in my Angell-infancy'.[11] Characteristically, Thomas mingles Christian metaphor and pagan nature-worship. In the fifth stanza the child continues happy 'as the heart was long', a reiterated but subtly modified phrase. Foxes and pheasants honour him in these bright farm landscapes, and one recalls Yeats's words 'meaning by vision the intense realization of a state of ecstatic emotion symbolized in a definite imagined region':[12]

> And honoured among foxes and pheasants by the gay house
> Under the new made clouds and happy as the heart was long,
> In the sun born over and over,
> I ran my heedless ways,
> My wishes raced through the house high hay
> And nothing I cared, at my sky blue trades, that time allows
> In all his tuneful turning so few and such morning songs
> Before the children green and golden
> Follow him out of grace.

For the child, however, there are now intimations of mortality, and the tide of ecstatic recollection begins to turn, the morning songs are few. The days of innocence – 'lamb white days' – give way to experience, knowledge of mortality, and the rising moon, the lengthening shadows, image this. One morning the farm will be bereft of the child, and childhood's vision:

> Nothing I cared, in the lamb white days, that time would take me
> Up to the swallow thronged loft by the shadow of my hand,
> In the moon that is always rising,
> Nor that riding to sleep
> I should hear him fly with the high fields
> And wake to the farm forever fled from the childless land.
> Oh as I was young and easy in the mercy of his means,
> Time held me green and dying
> Though I sang in my chains like the sea.

Singing, but in the chains of mortality, as the sea sings in its own chains of ebb and flow, an energy inexorably controlled, the poet ends with this sea-image that reverberates in the mind as did the earlier rhapsodic and lilting music. Thomas's concern to present nature in terms of heightened sensory perception is crystallized in the unbroken visionary landscapes of *Fern Hill*. It is against this achieved poetry of vision that we may set his youthful, perhaps callow and unfair, but not entirely unilluminating dismissal of the static element in Wordsworth's mystical poetry:

He writes about mysticism but he is not a mystic; he describes what mystics have been known to feel . . . He hadn't a spark of mysticism in him . . . And mysticism is illogical, unintellectual, and dogmatic.[13]

Clearly Thomas grasped the non-rational aspect of mystical experience; and emphasized the sense of energy rather than trance, the 'active participation'[14] in the experience his poems seek to create.

Plate 33. 'Fern Hill' as it is today.

There were over two hundred manuscript versions of *Fern Hill*, for after the addition or alteration of a single word or phrase Thomas would recopy the whole poem in longhand in order to keep the living growth of the poem. He often used separate worksheets for individual lines and the poem was built up, phrase by phrase, on a strict syllabic framework. It was indeed a craft, a hewn art, the sullen resistance of language, as of stone to carving, giving way finally to lilting cadences, many-layered verbal harmonies and associations. In a letter to Vernon Watkins in 1944 Thomas revealed his increasingly critical view of poetic composition and his clear-sighted judgement on his own development:

I'm so glad you wrote the last bit about the poems; how you so much more liked the latest to the earliest. Wouldn't it be hell if it was the other way round, and the words were coming quicker and slicker and weaker and wordier every day and, by comparison, one's first poems in adolescence seemed, to one, like flying-fish islands never to be born in again? Thank God, writing is daily more difficult, less passes Uncle Head's blue-haired pencil that George Q. Heart doesn't care about, and that the result, if only to you and me, is worth all the discarded shocks, the reluctantly shelved grand mooney images, cut-and-come again cardpack references.[15]

Thomas speaks here of a technical mastery, evident in all the later poems, critics have been slow or curiously reluctant to acknowledge.

A mile or two away from 'Fern Hill', in Blaen Cwm, was the stone cottage owned by Dylan's mother's brother, Tom Williams. Here Dylan often stayed, further absorbing the rural atmosphere and way of life of West Wales, so different from his home in suburban Swansea. Bored by the rain and the lack of convivial, talkative company, he writes to Pamela Hansford Johnson from this cottage – the year is 1933 – complaining that 'It is raining as I write, a thin purposeless rain hiding the long miles of desolate fields and scattered farmhouses. I can smell the river, and hear the beastly little brook that goes gingle-gingle past this room.'[16] Dylan seems well established as the favourite nephew for he continues, 'I am facing an uncomfortable fire, a row of china dogs, and a bureau bearing the photograph of myself aged seven – thick-lipped, Fauntleroy-haired, wide-eyed and empty as the bureau itself.' The books on the floor beside him include the prose of Donne and a 'Psychology of Insanity', while a nearby bookcase holds the Bible and a 'History of Welsh Castles'. He delights in giving what must have been a familiar enough episode an exaggeratedly macabre note, relating how a local man a few hours before had 'dropped the riddled bodies of eight rabbits on to the floor. He said it was good sport, shows me their torn

Plate 34. Blaen Cwm as it is now.

bellies and opened heads, brought out the ferret from his pocket for me to see. The ferret might have been his own child, he fondled it so. He called it "Billy Fach"'. It is with a more lyrical note, however, that he describes the journey he will later take to post the letter 'when it will be dark ... lamps will be lit in the farmhouses and the farmers will be sitting at their fires, looking into the blazing wood and thinking of God knows what littleness, or thinking of nothing at all but their own animal warmth.' Again this provides an interesting comparison with the later nostalgic recollections. Writing from Blaen Cwm in 1945, in contrast, Thomas's observation of the habits and foibles of the Welsh rural scene is not only acute but more compassionate. His impressions of the idiosyncrasies of place and character, of the deeply rooted habits of thought and feeling, were now raw material for his vision of Welsh life later to flower in *Under Milk Wood*:

It is hysterical weather where I am writing, Blaen Cwm, Llangain, Carmarthen, Wales, in a breeding-box in a cabbage valley in a parlour with a preserved sheepdog, where mothballs fly at night, not moths, where the Bible opens itself at Revelations; ... Gladys's pet lamb-now-sheep follows her maa'ing for poor, unloved Gladys's unmade milk ... Up the hill lane behind this house too full of Thomas's, a cottage row of undeniably mad or possessed peasantry of the

Plate 35. Family photograph 1936, with Pamela Hansford Johnson, Auntie Pollie, Dylan's mother, Uncle Dai (minister at Paraclete, Mumbles), Aunt Dosie Rees and Uncle Bob.

inbred crooked county, my cousins, uncles, aunts, the woman with the gooseberry birthmark who lies with dogs, the farm labourer who told me that the stream that runs by his cottage side is Jordan water and who can deny him, the lay preacher who believes the war was begun only to sell newspapers which are the devil's sermon-sheets.[17]

We see again the sacrosanct Welsh parlour, the Bible open at Revelations, while the reference to Jordan water recalls Mary Ann Sailor's conviction that Llareggub is both the promised land and the Garden of Eden. And does not the once kissed Bessie Bighead and her 'lake eyed cows' owe something to unloved Gladys and her pet sheep, and perhaps also to the birthmarked woman who 'lies with dogs'? It is not surprising that Thomas eulogized this countryside of West Wales so unequivocally, though characteristically with a pun on the word 'God':

> The country is holy: O bide in that country kind,
> Know the green good,

for it gave him inner vision and a distinctive social world he was to present with comedy and understanding, never harshly or sentimentally.

It was of course the nearby village of Laugharne, on the other side of the estuary, and where the life of the sea and country met, that produced the final – and tragically cut-off – flowering of Thomas's poetry and prose. In letters to Vernon Watkins written from Blaen Cwm in August 1944, Thomas spoke of 'a Laugharne poem: the first place poem I've written'.[18] It was *Poem in October* enclosed in the second letter with the comment 'It's got, I think, a lovely slow lyrical movement'[19] and the significant injunction 'Will you read it aloud too?'[19] It was Thomas's final rhapsodic evocation of childhood, before he moved to those poems of celebration and elegy that he called 'statements made on the way to the grave'.[20] Related in theme and technique to *Fern Hill* it, too, is a nostalgic recreation of visionary experience; for he often returned to Laugharne with its cliffside castle and hillsides sweeping to the sea's edge. In a letter to Margaret Taylor, written just before his move to the Boat House, Dylan shows how Laugharne was to him a timeless, lost Paradise, recalling

the clock of sweet Laugharne, the clock that tells the time backwards, so that soon, you walk through the town, from Browns to the gulls on the strand, in the only Golden Age! . . . and then, but only through my tears, the hundreds of years of the colossal broken castle, owls asleep in the centuries, the same rooks calling as in Arthur's time which always goes on there as, unborn, you climb the stones to see river, sea, cormorants nesting like thin headstones, the cockle-women webfoot, and the undead . . . the pubbed and churched, shopped, gulled, and estuaried one state of happiness.[21]

These scenes and sentiments are close to those of *Poem in October* as

Plate 36. Laugharne Castle.

early on the morning of his thirtieth birthday, he walks on the hillside above the village. The sounds of sea and seabirds and the tide's splash on boats and sea-wall greet his birthday stroll:

> It was my thirtieth year to heaven
> Woke to my hearing from harbour and neighbour wood
> And the mussel pooled and the heron
> Priested shore
> The morning beckon
> With water praying and call of seagull and rook
> And the knock of sailing boats on the net webbed wall
> Myself to set foot
> That second
> In the still sleeping town and set forth.

Sound, sight and movement fill this scene: the rooks in the trees, the boats bobbing against the sea-wall hung with fishing nets, the herons standing on one leg along the shore, priest-like in their solemn stance and as though giving benediction. The word 'Priested' to describe the heron, as they watch and stab the waters for fish, reminds us that along the Towy estuary – the setting of this poem – the fisherman kills his catch by tapping it on the head with a 'priest', the name here[22] for the implement that, as it were, administers the last rites.

As in *Fern Hill* Biblical language suggests the sacramental identity of the natural world: 'water praying', 'heron Priested' and later 'the parables of sun light' and 'legends of the green chapels' – for the country is holy; it is God's universe, however doubtful men's belief in priest, Bible story or chapel.

The birds of land and sea fly above the farms and sea waves as the poet commemorates his birthday, and October rain showers are transformed into the shower of past childhood days that fall as though from the sky. Interestingly, the original 'bare' trees Thomas changed to 'winged' – a metaphor suggesting the leafless branches are wings in flight like the birds that fly to them, a more dynamic image than the simply descriptive 'bare'. It is high tide, and the heron dives as the poet crosses the border of time, the awakening town below now closed to him:

> My birthday began with the water-
> Birds and the birds of the winged trees flying my name
> Above the farms and the white horses
> And I rose
> In rainy autumn
> And walked abroad in a shower of all my days
> High tide and the heron dived when I took the road

> Over the border
> And the gates
> Of the town closed as the town awoke

The poet climbs above the harbour 'dwindling' from sight below, the church like a snail from this distance, its tower horns through the early morning sea-borne mist ('sea-wet' describing the glistening wet church and also possibly a pun on 'sea-fret' – a term for sea-mist); and from here the castle ruins resemble the brown owls that frequent it. This language has intellectual exactitude as well as emotive and sensory power.

> Pale rain over the dwindling harbour
> And over the sea wet church the size of a snail
> With its horns through mist and the castle
> Brown as owls

Interestingly, this *Poem in October* walk follows the shore-line around the mud-flats, going away from the Boat House, and today there is a wooden stile on the sea-edge of the wood. One then enters a charming heavily-wooded dingle, and beyond this, to the right, can be seen an old orchard containing a number of fruit trees, including apples. There are also 'red currants' in the form of hoar berries and mulberries. Turning up the hill, the higher slopes afford the view of Laugharne which corresponds to the description in the poem.

At this point the poet turns from this rainy scene, moving from time present to time past ('beyond the border') visiting again the spring and summer landscapes of childhood, albeit idealized, the exaggerated ('tall') tales. The word 'But' here points the contrast between the actual rainy weather of the present and the 'summer' weather of the childhood vision:

> But all the gardens
> Of spring and summer were blooming in the tall tales
> Beyond the border and under the lark full cloud.

He sees again as he saw as a boy, and the timeless landscapes of light and summer flow past, stunningly sustained by Thomas's command of rhythm and image:

> And down the other air and the blue altered sky
> Streamed again a wonder of summer
> With apples
> Pears and red currants
> And I saw in the turning so clearly a child's
> Forgotten mornings when he walked with his mother

> Through the parables
> Of sun light
> And the legends of the green chapels

Through tears that belong to the boy he was, he experiences the feelings of childhood anew:

> And the twice told fields of infancy
> That his tears burned my cheeks and his heart moved in mine.

The child's mystical sense of communion with nature is repeated in the adult poet's vision. The dead become the listening 'undead', as evoked in the timeless world of the Laugharne letter. The mystery of the boy's empathy with the natural world is recreated:

> These were the woods the river and sea
> Where a boy
> In the listening
> Summertime of the dead whispered the truth of his joy
> To the trees and the stones and the fish in the tide.
> And the mystery
> Sang alive
> Still in the water and singing birds.

The poem reaches its climax in lines of remarkable simplicity, as the true joy of the child the poet once was lives again; Vaughan's 'bright shoots of everlastingness'[11] and Wordsworth's 'the glory and the dream'[23] dramatically and lyrically achieved:

> And the true
> Joy of the long dead child sang burning
> In the sun.

The poem closes on a note of hiraeth, that Welsh sense of nostalgia, as the poet expresses his longing that he may, in a year's time ('turning') celebrate the 'heart's truth' on this same hill, despite the shed blood of passing time:

> It was my thirtieth
> Year to heaven stood there then in the summer noon
> Though the town below lay leaved with October blood
> O may my heart's truth
> Still be sung
> On this high hill in a year's turning

As in the alteration of 'bare' to 'winged' Thomas's substitute of the initial 'was brown' to 'lay leaved' indicates the device whereby the change of a word or phrase enriches the life of the whole line. The image of the town strewn with fallen leaves is both precisely and movingly evoked in the final phrase chosen, with its autumnal echoes of other lives and other poems.

It is well to remember that it was in his thirties that Thomas wrote his most notable poems, a period that begins with *Poem in October* (finished a few weeks before his birthday) and includes *A Refusal to Mourn*, *Fern Hill* and *A Winter's Tale*. Thomas was not to live permanently in Laugharne until the spring of 1949, when Margaret Taylor generously bought the Boat House for Dylan and his family; he settled his parents in a nearby cottage called 'The Pelican' opposite Brown's Hotel. A letter of thanks shows how grateful Dylan was to be able to return 'to this place I love'.[24] The poet simply but profoundly registers his sense of renewal, of a 'fresh beginning'.[24] His tribute to Margaret Taylor was a moving one: 'All I shall write in this water and tree room on the cliff, every word will be a thanks to you.'[24] It was a promise of composition he was to keep, the happiest and most fruitful of his remaining years spent in that now fabled 'water and tree room on the cliff'.

Plate 37. Dylan's writing shed.

PART IV

Laugharne: 'Druid in his own Land'[1]

'God is the country of the spirit'[2]

The village of Laugharne is built on hill-slopes which descend to the seashore, hills that almost meet as they sweep down on either side of the horseshoe bay. The small town square is bordered on one side by the stretches of sand and mud flats, and the tidal estuary looks out to Carmarthen Bay. In the square is the Cross House Inn and close by, up the sloping street and just past the small town hall is Brown's Hotel, these the two pubs that Thomas frequented. Just off the square and looking out to sea across the long stretches of mud flats stands Laugharne Castle. Further along the bay, stretching out from the cliffside to the sea, is the Boat House. Half way up the cliff path, which leads from the village to the Boat House, is Thomas's workshop – his 'water and tree room on the cliff' also called by him affectionately 'the shack'. It looks from the outside much like a small garage; perched like a bird's nest precariously on the high cliff, exposed to the storms and sea-noises, winds and weather of the estuary. Its two large, picture windows overlooked the life of the bay, the trailing greenery of leaves and brambles growing about it. Furnished with bare wooden table, chairs, and anthracite stove, the room was apt to become itself a sea of manuscripts, discarded drafts of poems, empty cigarette packets, literary periodicals, and books.

The path at this point narrows as it slopes up to the Boat House, and is flanked on one side by the trees and bushes growing out of the cliff-face. In spring and summer wild flowers crowd this side of the path. On its other side, gaps in the hedgerow reveal the sea which laps against this mountain wall when the tide is in. The pathway, thus overlooking the sea and mud flats, seems hewn out of the green hillside. Beginning at the gate, a garden slopes down to the Boat House, reversing the journey of the cliff path. The Boat House is built halfway up the cliff, and the house with its verandah over the sea wall seems to grow out of the rock. Walking on this verandah, which runs along two sides of the house, seems at night like walking on the deck of a ship, the sea awash

Plate 38. The entrance of the Boat House.

below and the lights of the 'sheepwhite hollow farms' across the estuary like the lights of ships in the distance.

I recall Vernon Watkins saying in conversation that Yeats had taught the lyric poet to grow old. Dylan Thomas returned to Laugharne at the approach of middle age when, following Yeats's triumphant example, this lyric poet too was learning to grow old. In his last years Thomas was writing verse confronting the problems of age as passionate, vigorous, and original as that recording his youthful obsessions. It is true that in the last six years of his life Dylan Thomas wrote only seven poems, but these were all major poems: *In Country Sleep, Over Sir John's Hill, In the White Giant's Thigh, Lament, Do not go gentle into that good night, Poem on his Birthday, Author's Prologue*. It is a considerable poetic achievement in six years – whichever poet writing in English is chosen for comparison! Additionally, the unfinished poems *In Country Heaven* and *Elegy* have the simplicity and imaginative power of his finest verse. These, too, were the years that produced *Under Milk Wood*, further broadcast talks like *A Visit to America*, remarkable tales like *The Followers* and *A Story*. He also continued the flow of letters – often intoxicating fantasies and vivid arias of comedy made from what

87

were usually statements of penury and recitals of those despairs, worries, frustrations that were the darker, more familiar, daily side of the gold coin of poetic vision. This was achieved despite the killing interruptions of the American tours when, as Dylan so rightly said, 'I can only play a poet there, and not make poetry'.[3] To see Dylan Thomas's last years as marking a diminution of poetic power is contrary to all the evidence; it is a false legend that confuses the problems of the life with creative challenges Thomas was facing and surmounting. Undoubtedly the essential development in Thomas's poetry was the growth from introspective stasis, passionately discovering the world in the map of his own body, to the universality of the sculptured vision. The stern but compassionate romanticism of the 'hewn' voice that rings through these later poems recording Thomas's deepening vision of the unity-in-duality of man and nature, is that of the (again) Yeatsian ideal of 'our delight in the whole man – blood, imagination, intellect, running together'.[4] Beyond English gentility and its counterpoint of a modish violence, it is a vision ultimately harmonious and healing. Mutability, age, and death are confronted, and overcome. And the sea and landscapes of this corner of Wales, Laugharne in particular, are scene and inspiration of this achievement.

'Sir John's Hill is a real hill overlooking an estuary in West Wales'[5] was Dylan's introduction to his B.B.C. reading of *Over Sir John's Hill* in 1950, and the seascape and hill could be seen from the window of the poet's 'water and tree room'. It is a narrative poem describing a hawk killing its prey, and it is clear how the poem began: a hawk seeking its prey must have been a common enough event:

> Over Sir John's hill,
> The hawk on fire hangs still

'on fire' visually evokes the sunlight on its wings and suggests too its potential for destruction: the hawk is a killer who

> pulls to his claws
> And gallows, up the rays of eyes the small birds of the bay

To speak of his claws as gallows continues the metaphor of execution as the doomed, warring, wrangling birds sing their last:

> Wars
> Of the sparrows and such who swansing, dusk, in wrangling hedges.

The hawk with the noose and the hill that is 'fiery tyburn' are the agent

Plate 39. The estuary and Sir John's Hill.

and place of execution/punishment. The movement of the verse here enacts the swoop of the hawk, but after the kill assumes an elegiac rhythm. A new figure, the heron, fishing in the river Towy that flows into the estuary, enters the scene, observer and memorialist as his head dips into the water:

> And blithely they squawk
> To fiery tyburn over the wrestle of elms until
> The flash, the noosed hawk
> Crashes, and slowly the fishing holy stalking heron
> In the river Towy below bows his tilted headstone

We may recall Dylan's 'cormorants nesting like thin headstones' in the earlier Laugharne letter. The just hill, covered with jackdaws, is said to wear the black cap of a judge passing sentence of death on these noisy, 'gulled' birds, an image both visual and allegorical as it implies their guilt:

> Flash, and the plumes crack
> And a black cap of jack-
> Daws Sir John's just hill dons,

The heron is now the 'elegiac fisherbird' and the invitation 'Come and be killed', suggests the inevitability of the action, as the poet enters the narrative. He is reading in nature the book of life 'the leaves of the water' – which in turn suggests the leaves of a tree, a characteristic merging and uniting of the forms of natural life. The act of killing the poet witnesses is itself part of the processes of nature. Not life, but the form of life ends and changes:

> There
> Where the elegiac fisherbird stabs and paddles
> In the pebbly dab-filled
> Shallow and sedge, and 'dilly dilly', calls the loft hawk,
> 'Come and be killed,'
> I open the leaves of the water at a passage
> Of psalms and shadows among the pincered sandcrabs prancing

The poet is reconciled to death, reading it in a shell, the husk of a once living creature; and at this moment, sea-sounds of the buoy's bell suggest a funeral bell. 'All praise' is given to 'the hawk on fire', for it is performing its natural function, a function the poet accepts and celebrates:

> And read, in a shell,
> Death clear as a buoy's bell:
> All praise of the hawk on fire in hawk-eyed dusk be sung.

Like the heron, the poet remains outside the action; but he adopts a bardic and prophetic stance, interceding on behalf of the life it is his role to celebrate and commemorate:

> It is the heron and I, under judging Sir John's elmed
> Hill, tell-tale the knelled
> Guilt
> Of the led-astray birds whom God, for their breast of whistles,
> Have mercy on,
> God in his whirlwind silence save, who marks the sparrows hail,
> For their souls' song.

There are obvious Biblical echoes and rhythms in the supplication for mercy, and in the reference to the sparrows. One recalls Thomas's statement that the Bible's 'great stories of Noah, Jonah, Lot, Moses, Jacob, Solomon . . . I had, of course, known from very early youth; the great rhythms had rolled over me from the Welsh Pulpits . . . and the story of the New Testament is part of my life.'[6] Importantly, it is remembered not studied, for he further declared that 'All of the Bible that I use in my work is remembered from childhood.'

Death dominates the final stanza, slowing the cadences of the verse and determining the selection of image: 'tear of the Towy', 'Wear-willow river'. The elms are 'looted' now that life has been destroyed, and the poet acknowledges himself no less vulnerable than the birds to 'the lunge of the night'. As one carving on stone he writes, making his ritual of remembrance, though performing rites that time will erase. The sweep and passion of these lines is combined with the detail and precision of a sculptured frieze. We see the dusk falling, the heron's movement mirrored in the waters, the snapt feathers like snow in the gathering dark; yet the scene has also the marmoreal stillness of elegy. The verse achieves the 'cold and passionate'[7] poetic ideal shared by Yeats:

> Now the heron grieves in the weeded verge. Through windows
> Of dusk and water I see the tilting whispering
> Heron, mirrored, go
> As the snapt feathers snow,
> Fishing in the tear of the Towy. Only a hoot owl
> Hollows, a grassblade blown in cupped hands, in the looted elms
> And no green cocks or hens
> Shout
> Now on Sir John's hill. The heron, ankling the scaly
> Lowlands of the waves,
> Makes all the music; and I who hear the tune of the slow,
> Wear-willow river, grave,

Plate 40. The Boat House.

> Before the lunge of the night, the notes on this time-shaken
> Stone for the sake of the souls of the slain birds sailing.

Only an owl's cry and sounds of flowing water break the silence as night falls on trees and heron, sea-waves, and poet. Common enough events as Thomas walked the cliff path home at night, they are here wrought into the conclusion of a formal elegy, the final lilting cadences of an allegory of the human condition.

Also inspired by the Laugharne sea-scape, *Author's Prologue* is more directly and simply descriptive of the setting. The poet is looking out at sunset from his home above the bay, and sees the summer's end, fishermen at their nets, sandboys at play, herons and shells. Though the poet writes 'at poor peace', his art is sacred, and he compares himself to Noah. He is building an ark of poetry into which he invites all the creatures of Wales, of its seas, its woods and its countryside. This ark is a symbol of love, and the poet glories in the world, which is man-torn yet blessed by his blood. The whole world of nature, bird, fish, and animal is greeted and welcomed. The poem closes with a description of the Ark riding out under the stars of Wales.

So relentlessly did Dylan Thomas correct and recorrect his work, there were over 160 manuscript versions of the *Prologue*; and this despite the urgent calls of the publishers for its completion, for it was holding up publication of Thomas's *Collected Poems*. As he explains in a letter he worked for two months on the poem to achieve the difficult technical task he set himself. The poem consists of 102 lines, the first rhyming with the last, the second with the last but one, the third with the last but two, and so on until the middle where two rhymes meet.

Though desperately short of money, Thomas would not hurry the completion of the poem, neither did he turn to more commercially lucrative writing. Nor did he of course compromise by writing a more easily completed preface. Undoubtedly, in these later years he composed less in any given period of time, owing to the greater critical effort he put into his work. During the long concentrated, isolated months of composition in Laugharne, Thomas was able to work without distraction. Caitlin Thomas in her book *Leftover Life to Kill* has successfully shown the close bond between the poet and this, for him, nourishing Welsh environment.

And I did all I could to make him work, at his own special work and not the public money-making work. And it was only with our kind of purely vegetable background, which entailed months on end of isolated, stodgy dullness and drudgery for me, that he was flattened out enough to be able to concentrate.[8]

Dylan's way of life followed a working-class, rather than a middle-class pattern: drinking with local friends in the pub, sharing their interests and gossip, being in fact one of them, looking and behaving like anyone else in the village. He fitted easily and comfortably into the Laugharne setting, working steadily and concentratedly every afternoon in his 'shack'. Dylan's wife has given a vivid account of his daily routine, describing the regularly industrious, yet relaxed life he enjoyed there:

So he was much better than me at contenting himself with the very simple, I might justly say moronic, life. Because, there is no other possible explanation, he lived in a world of his own: 'out of this world' as they so succinctly put it in America. Thus: the best part of the morning in the kitchen of this same high class establishment (the Brown's Hotel), putting bets on horses, listening, yes, actually listening for once, open mouthed, to local gossip and scandal, while drinking slow consecutive pints. Muzzily back to late lunch, of one of our rich fatty brews, always eaten alone, apart from the children ... then up to his humble shed, nesting high above the estuary; and bang into intensive scribbling, muttering, whispering, intoning, bellowing and juggling of words; till seven o'clock prompt.
Then straight back to one of the alternative dumps (the pubs).[9]

Plate 41. Brown's Hotel, Laugharne.

Plate 42. Dylan drinking in Brown's Hotel.

Thomas's interests were not those of the literary intellectual or cosmopolitan bohemian writer: literary parties, the theatre, discussions, there were none of these in Laugharne. Few contemporary poets can have lived such a hum-drum life; even his drinking, though regular, was in Laugharne, steady rather than excessive! Daily, with an almost Victorian filial devotion, he visited his parents, doing the crossword with his father and exchanging news and gossip. In his broadcast talk on Laugharne he writes with fondness and a deep sense of belonging that

Off and on, up and down, high and dry, man and boy, I've been living now for fifteen years, or centuries, in this timeless, beautiful, barmy (both spellings) town, in this far forgetful, important place of herons, cormorants, castle, church yard, gulls, ghosts.

A playful humour soon further enlivens the description, when Thomas declares he 'can claim to be able to call several of the inhabitants, and a few of the herons, by their Christian names'.

As Dylan Thomas worked in his cliffside shed overlooking sea and countryside, or walked the winding path down to the village and the deeply enjoyed social pleasures of the pub, he was safe in the daily care and love of his family and village friends. It was clear that Laugharne was the safe womb/island, what he calls 'this timeless, mild, beguiling island of a town'. And reading his last poems one has a sense of his solitary absorption in this place, a sense too of a man communing most deeply with the life of nature – a world whose reality (in contrast to the American lecture tours and his adopted role of entertainer) immediately supported and fruitfully engulfed him:

> In the mustardseed sun,
> By full tilt river and switchback sea
>   Where the cormorants scud,
> In his house on stilts high among beaks
>   And palavers of birds
> This sandgrain day in the bent bay's grave
>   He celebrates and spurns
> His driftwood thirty-fifth wind turned age;
>   Herons spire and spear.

Thus the opening of another birthday poem, his thirty-fifth, as he watches the herons and gulls, the hawks and fishes, all hunting for their prey and whose death is shown as part of the scheme of things. From his cliffside vantage-point, 'his house on stilts', on a day that is but a sandgrain beside the total immensity of time, the world of the bay is viewed as a graveyard in which every living thing moves towards death:

> Under and round him go
> Flounders, gulls, on their cold, dying trails,
>   Doing what they are told,
> Curlews aloud in the congered waves
>   Work at their ways to death,
> And the rhymer in the long tongued room,
>   Who tolls his birthday bell,
> Toils towards the ambush of his wounds;
>   Herons, steeple stemmed, bless.

The herons are emblematic yet at the same time living and dying birds, and the poet, as in *Over Sir John's hill* and *Author's Prologue*, is witness and celebrator of the scene. Thomas's earlier obsession with the mortality of his own body has become the wider, calmer sense of a doom shared with natural life in 'the bent bay's grave', and the Laugharne sea-scape, a shared grave, becomes the one world of man and

Plate 43. The Pelican, Dylan's parents' home in Laugharne.

nature on their voyage to death. 'The ambush of his wounds' towards
which 'the rhymer ... toils' refers to the act of redemption that the
poet, in his art, performs, that art being itself a rite and ritual. Finches
and fishes pass before him inexorably to their death:

> In the thistledown fall,
> He sings towards anguish; finches fly
> In the claw tracks of hawks
> On a seizing sky; small fishes glide
> Through wynds and shells of drowned
> Ship towns to pastures of otters. He
> In his slant, racking house
> And the hewn coils of his trade perceives
> Herons walk in their shroud,

The past life of the bay is evoked in 'wynds' and 'drowned/Ship
towns'; and there is a similar vision of time past in a later stanza, and
an evocation too of future destruction and change. When writing this
stanza I believe Dylan Thomas had in mind the prehistoric Coygan
cave, off the Pendine road out of Laugharne, which is remarkable,
archaeologically, for its rich deposits of mammoth, woolly rhinoceros,
and other long extinct animals.

> There he might wander bare
> With the spirits of the horseshoe bay
> Or the stars' seashore dead,
> Marrow of eagles, the roots of whales
> And wishbones of wild geese,
> ....
> Who knows the rocketing wind will blow
> The bones out of the hills,
> And the scythed boulders bleed......

Though the poet laments the vicissitudes of life's deathward jour-
ney:

> Oh, let me midlife mourn by the shrined
> And druid herons' vows
> The voyage to ruin I must run,

yet he rejects the nihilism, despair and pessimism that so much twen-
tieth century writing has voiced. Accepting his own anguish and un-
certainty, he reaches beyond this to celebrate the facts of humanity and
the natural universe, and the survival of the spirit of love:

> Yet, though I cry with tumbledown tongue,
> Count my blessings aloud:

Four elements and five
Senses, and man a spirit in love

The poet has learned to accept even the terms of his own inner conflict. He has learned 'to praise in spite of'. As he approaches death, Thomas celebrates a universe that seems even more worthy of praise. It is not the dark journey to oblivion, autumnal and wintry, of D. H. Lawrence's 'Ship of Death', but a journey in brightening sunlight on an exulting sea, with a final sense not of isolation, but of unity:

. . . the closer I move
To death, one man through his sundered hulks,
The louder the sun blooms
And the tusked, ramshackling sea exults . . . .
. . . . the whole world then,
With more triumphant faith
Than ever was since the world was said,
Spins its morning of praise . . . .

The drawing of a lighthouse on an island, the tower and rays blacked in, and the comment 'Darkhouse' appears on one of the worksheets of this poem.[10] I am indebted to Maureen Duffy for her shrewd realization that this is the probable source of 'mansouled fiery islands' and 'my shining men', for as the poet sails seawards to death, lighthouses and their keepers aptly continue this metaphor of the journey: images not of terror and oblivion but of the light and love of men shining in the dark. 'The small, bonebound island', as the poet spoke of himself in youth, has reached the wider vision of 'The mansouled fiery islands':

. . . . and how
More spanned with angels ride
The mansouled fiery islands! Oh,
Holier then their eyes,
And my shining men no more alone
As I sail out to die.

The worksheets of this poem indicate the jigsaw-like pattern of Thomas's method of composition. Words and phrases are altered to fit the pattern of thought; thus, 'shambling sky' becomes 'seizing sky' in the finished poem, 'spiralling cloud' becomes 'serpent cloud'; 'Herons, on one leg, bless' becomes 'Herons, steeple stemmed, bless'. Sometimes the word lists on the worksheets catalogue possible rhymes: ball, call, crawl, haul, squall, trawl, wall. It is clear the poet explores and toys with certain images and words. As in the case of manuscript worksheets of Yeats's poetry, the original version tends to differ from the final one mainly in stylistic expression rather than theme, often reading like a rough paraphrase of the final poem. In one version for example most of the expressions were rejected, though they conform with the rest of the poem in terms of idea, such as the lines:

> At half his bible span,
> A man of words who'd drag down the stars to his lyric oven,
> He looks back at his years.

(from worksheets of *Poem on his birthday* reproduced in the present author's *Dylan Thomas: His Life and Work*).

Caitlin Thomas has given this authentic account of her husband's method of composition:

And dear God, when I think of that concentrated muttering, and mumbling, and intoning, the realms of discarded lists of rhyming words, the innumerable repetitions and revisions, and how at the end of an intensive five-hour stretch (from two to seven prompt as clockwork) Dylan would come out very pleased with himself saying, he had done a good day's work – and present me proudly with one or two, or three perhaps, fiercely belaboured lines[11]

In his 'Note' to the *Collected Poems* Thomas declared that 'These poems, with all their crudities, doubts and confusions, are written for the love of Man and in praise of God.' Bearing in mind his reported comment they were 'poems in praise of God's world by a man who doesn't believe in God',[12] the word 'doubts' is important, implying as it does the quest and exploration, rather than the certain faith, of religious verse. In his early poem *And death shall have no dominion* death was vanquished not by faith ('Faith in their hands shall snap in two'), but by nature:

> Heads of the characters hammer through daisies

a poetic statement of the familiar and colloquial 'pushing up the daisies'. In *Poem on his birthday*, Thomas's last completed poem, it is still the paradox of belief and unbelief that haunts him, a God loved yet fabled rather than known, a heaven both without existence yet held to be true:

> And freely he goes lost
> In the unknown, famous light of great
> And fabulous, dear God.
> Dark is a way and light is a place,
> Heaven that never was
> Nor will be ever is always true,

The picture of Dylan Thomas I am left with is of a man wrestling

Plate 44. Writing in the shed.

with belief and unbelief, yet finally settled in neither. His poetry distills the tension of an imagination haunted by religious faith and identities, yet certain only of the realities of the physical universe. Chief of these realities is death.

There is a significant development in the role of nature in Thomas's last poems, an imaginative purpose the poet spoke of in his introduction to a reading in 1950 of the completed poems that formed 'separate parts of a long poem'[13] in preparation, provisionally titled *In Country Heaven*. 'The Poem', Thomas states, 'becomes . . . . . an affirmation of the beautiful and terrible worth of the Earth. It grows into a praise of what is and could be on this lump in the skies.'[14] The emphasis is on *this* world, the physical universe. However, Thomas's presentation of nature is directed by a concept of time whereby physical immediacy effects an 'active participation',[14] though the poem may be one of recollection, prophecy, or divination. 'The remembered tellings,' declares the poet, 'are not all told as though they are remembered . . . The memory, in all tenses, can look towards the future, can caution and admonish. The rememberer may live himself back into active participation in the remembered scene, adventure, or spiritual condition.'[14] Thomas had anticipated this presentation of the natural world in the poems of childhood, and also in *A Winter's Tale*, which is an expansive and lyrical evocation of country life in winter:

> And the stars falling cold,
> And the smell of hay in the snow, and the far owl
> Warning among the folds, and the frozen hold
> Flocked with the sheep white smoke of the farm house cowl
> In the river wended vales where the tale was told.

And significantly, at the moment of prayer for love:

> Deliver him, he cried,
> By losing him all in love,

Nature comes mystically alive from the past:

> . . . . The nightingale,
> Dust in the buried wood, flies on the grains of her wings
> . . . .
> . . . . . The wizened
> Stream with bells and baying water bounds. The dew rings
> On the gristed leaves and the long gone glistening
> Parish of snow. The carved mouths in the rock are wind swept
> strings.

In this revivified natural world, it is the she-bird, symbolizing love, which rises; and the 'intricately' dead come miraculously to life in delicate and precisely knit images:

> Look. And the dancers move
> On the departed, snow bushed green, wanton in moon light
> As a dust of pigeons, Exulting, the grave hooved
> Horses, centaur dead, turn and tread the drenched white
> Paddocks in the farms of birds. The dead oak walks for love.
>
> The carved limbs in the rock
> Leap, as to trumpets. Calligraphy of the old
> Leaves is dancing.

In the moment of vision 'the time dying flesh' is overcome.

In Country Sleep, one of the completed poems in the projected *In Country Heaven* sequence, is addressed to the poet's young daughter, and he tells her not to fear the fictions of folk tales or stories told her before sleep:

> Never and never, my girl riding far and near
> In the land of the hearthstone tales, and spelled asleep,
> Fear or believe that the wolf in a sheepwhite hood
> Loping and bleating roughly and blithely shall leap . . .
> To eat your heart in the house in the rosy wood.

Nor should she grow to fear sexuality:

> . . . no gooseherd or swine will turn
> Into a homestall king or hamlet of fire
>   And prince of ice
> To court the honeyed heart from your side . . . .

for she is shielded in her *Country Sleep*: there is security in nature:

> From the broomed witch's spume you are shielded by fern
> And flower of country sleep and the greenwood keep.

The child's fear of sleep and dreams (fictions) should be forgotten since only death itself threatens, 'the stern Bell' that echoes, and 'the Thief' who moves in time through the poem:

> Never, my girl, until tolled to sleep by the stern
>
> Bell believe or fear that the rustic shade or spell
> Shall harrow and snow the blood . . .

It is death, not experience or sexuality, who is the constant Thief that merits fear:

Plate 45. Dylan and family in Laugharne: standing, Dylan and Llewelyn; seated, Aeronwy, Dylan's mother, Colm and Caitlin.

Fear most

For ever of all not the wolf in his baaing hood
Nor the tusked prince, in the ruttish farm, at the rind
And mire of love, but the Thief meek as the dew.

With subtly evocative images drawn from the natural world the poet suggests the unperceived but inevitable approach of death, 'the sly and sure' Thief who, since the child's birth, has been visitor:

> Ever and ever he finds a way, as the snow falls,
>
> As the rain falls, hail on the fleece, as the vale mist rides
> Through the haygold stalls . . . . .

The poem concludes with the idea that in the cycle of nature death brings re-immersion into the natural world and what is lost (i.e. death steals or takes away) is only the belief that a heaven or hell follows. Contrastingly, Yeats's *A Prayer for my Daughter* warns of the social and psychological perils life might bring; ceremony, custom and moderation being the safeguards. For Thomas, it is in nature that trust must be placed:

> The country is holy: O bide in that country kind,
> > Know the green good.

In the white giant's thigh, also belonging to the sequence *In Country Heaven*, and *Elegy*, the unfinished poem Thomas was writing to commemorate his father, both explore man's soul as being born from nature and returning to it in death after a period when the soul lingers in memory. In *In the white giant's thigh* the longing of the women to love and conceive is expressed in terms of the creative energy of the natural world:

> Through throats where many rivers meet, the curlews cry,
> Under the conceiving moon, on the high chalk hill,
> And there this night I walk in the white giant's thigh
> Where barren as boulders women lie longing still
> To labour and love though they lay down long ago.

When writing this poem it is probable Dylan Thomas had in mind the white giant on the upper slopes of a high chalk hill, known appropriately as Giant Hill, overlooking the Dorset village of Cerne Abbas. This remarkable hill figure, cut in the turf, is thought to be of Romano-British origins, and is clearly a pagan fertility symbol. In his right hand the giant carries a cudgel, but more striking is the prodigiously erect penis. There is a local tradition that copulation on the grass within the phallus is a cure for barrenness in women. Significantly, too, the phallus points exactly to the spot where the sun would come over the crest of the hill on May Day. Dylan Thomas must certainly have known of this Giant, and in all likelihood visited Cerne Abbas when he

THE GIANT, CERNE ABBAS   PR.4960

Plate 46. The Giant, Cerne Abbas.

106

lived in Ringwood, some twenty miles to the east on the Dorset and Hampshire border.

The desires and emotions of women are spoken of as remaining after death and even beyond memory:

> Through throats where many rivers meet, the women pray,
> Pleading in the waded bay for the seed to flow
> Though the names on their weed grown stones are rained away.

It is as though the curlew's cry embodies their eternal yearning for the unconceived sons on this – significantly – 'cudgelling, hacked Hill':

> And alone in the night's eternal, curving act
> They yearn with tongues of curlews for the unconceived
> And immemorial sons of the cudgelling, hacked
> Hill.

Though the women's grave stones are covered in fallen leaves and grass, names and epitaphs worn away, the poet writes of their love as eternally existing in nature; and it is this 'evergreen' love that he seeks:

> Teach me the love that is evergreen after the fall leaved
> Grave, after Belovéd on the grass gulfed cross is scrubbed
> Off by the sun and Daughters no longer grieved
> Save by their long desires . . . . . .

The poem concludes:

> And the daughters of darkness flame like Fawkes fires still.

The two poems Thomas wrote on his father in these last years show, I think, a simplicity in their nevertheless unremitting artifice that may owe something to the influence of his dramatic writing in prose and poetry, where the need to be immediately understood was paramount. There is an elegance in the structure of *Do not go gentle into that good night* that has perhaps gone largely unnoticed due to the intensity of the anguish and anger that the poem so eloquently records. Thomas's father was dying from cancer of the throat, going blind just before he died on 16 December – a date approaching the shortest ('darkest') day. There is a Yeatsian protest at old age and death, so that 'good night' becomes the everyday but overwhelming metaphor of death:

> Do not go gentle into that good night,
> Old age should burn and rave at close of day;
> Rage, rage against the dying of the light.

The reiterated 'rage', together with the paradoxical 'good night', the key words in the poem, strongly recalls the similar language and situation of Yeats's poem *The Choice:*

> The intellect of man is forced to choose
> Perfection of the life, or of the work,
> And if it choose the latter, must refuse
> A heavenly mansion, raging in the dark.[15]

Though unlike Yeats in that he never quite dismisses the 'heavenly mansion' and confidently proclaims the light – and in this unlike his own dying father it seems – Thomas, like Yeats, chose perfection of the work rather than the life and 'rages' against death in his moods of personal protest and anguish – particularly, as here, when faced with the death of those he loved. Again like Yeats, Thomas proclaims not the 'gravitas' of priests but the 'tragic gaiety' that goes on building despite destruction and death:

> Grave men, near death, who see with blinding sight
> Blind eyes could blaze like meteors and be gay,
> Rage, rage against the dying of the light.

'Blaze' and 'gay' of course bring to mind Yeats's *Lapis Lazuli*, a poem that faces the inevitability of the destruction of man and his works:

> Gaiety transfiguring all that dread . . . .
> Black out; Heaven blazing into the head,[16]

but celebrates the tragic delight of those who behold this but are steadfast:

> Their eyes, mid many wrinkles, their eyes,
> Their ancient, glittering eyes, are gay.

Like Yeats's *The Choice, Do not go gentle* is comprised of ten syllable lines, but Thomas weaves the tapestry of passionate protest in three line stanzas, employing only two rhymes throughout, in this villanelle of appropriately nineteen lines, and repeating the opening line of stanza one to close stanzas two and four, while the last line of stanza one is repeated to close stanzas three and five, these two magnificently echoing lines meeting in the concluding stanza. I think Thomas's achievement as a poet lies in this fusion of artifice and passion. In the later unfinished *Elegy*, written after his father's death, the three line structure of the stanza is set against a four line rhyme scheme (abab, cdcd), so that a craftsman's artifice sustains the impassioned grief and harrowing sense of loss the poem records:

> Out of his eyes I saw the last light glide.
> Here among the light of the lording sky
> An old man is with me where I go

> Walking in the meadows of his son's eye
> On whom a world of ills came down like snow.
> He cried as he died, fearing at last the spheres'
>
> Last sound, the world going out without a breath . . .
>
> O deepest wound of all that he should die
> On that darkest day.

As in *Do not go gentle* a basic but rare simplicity of structure is accompanied by tellingly simple language; suggesting again not failing inspiration but new directions of poetic development. As in *In the white giant's thigh* but more personally and intimately in this *Elegy* for his father, the poet suggests a continuing of love and renewed life in nature:

> Oh, forever may
> He lie lightly, at last, on the last, crossed
> Hill, under the grass, in love, and there grow
>
> Young among the long flocks and never lie lost
> Or still all the numberless days of his death . . . .

The poet images the very process of dying as a return to nature:

> The rivers of the dead
>
> Veined his poor hand I held, and I saw
> Through his unseeing eyes to the roots of the sea,

while he himself will be forever haunted by his father's presence as he is by God's:

> I am not too proud to cry that He and he
> Will never never go out of my mind.

In these last years Dylan Thomas was also maturing his gifts as an artist in comedy. Most of this was commissioned work, much of it for the B.B.C., such as *A Story* and *Under Milk Wood*. *A Story* hilariously describes 'a day's outing, by charabanc, to Porthcawl, which, of course, the charabanc never reached'. This tale of a typically Welsh drinking trip Thomas wrote for television just after going on such an outing from Laugharne. As so often in his stories he gives a child's eye view:

'If you go on that outing on Saturday, Mr Thomas,' she (Mrs Thomas) said to my uncle in her small, silk voice, 'I'm going home to my mother's.'

Holy Mo, I thought, she's got a mother . . . . .
'It's me or the outing, Mr Thomas.'

I would have made my choice at once, but it was almost half
a minute before my uncle said: 'Well then, Sarah, it's the
outing, my love.' He lifted her up, under his arm, on to a
chair in the kitchen, and she hit him on the head with the china
dog. Then he lifted her down again, and then I said goodnight.

A Story is more true to Wales than Wales itself, as Thomas's handling
of dialogue, for which he obviously had an acute ear and retentive

Plate 47. In Laugharne churchyard shortly after the death of his father.

memory, is clear and dramatic; while the narrative moves in a lively yet leisurely way:

'What can we do with him (the boy now accompanying the men),
when we stop for refreshments?' . . . . .
'Twenty-six minutes to opening time,' shouted an old man in
a panama hat, not looking at his watch. They forgot me at once.
'Good old Mr Cadwalladwr,' they cried, and the charabanc
started off down the village street.
A few cold women stood at their doorways, grimly watching us go.
A very small boy waved good-bye, and his mother boxed his ears.
It was a beautiful August morning.

Thus the comedy is touched by moments of pathos, and the varying notes are struck by deft metaphor and apt rhythms:

We were out of the village, and over the bridge, and up the
hill towards Steeplehat Wood when Mr Franklyn, with his list
of names in his hand, called out loud:
'Where's old O. Jones?'
'Where's old O.?'
'We've left old O. behind.'
'Can't go without old O'.
And though Mr Weazley hissed all the way, we turned and drove back to the village, where outside the Prince of Wales, old O. Jones was waiting patiently and alone with a canvas bag.
'I didn't want to come at all,' old O. Jones said as they hoisted him into the charabanc and clapped him on the back and pushed him on a seat and stuck a bottle in his hand, 'but I always go.'
And over the bridge and up the hill and under the deep green wood and along the dusty road we wove, slow cows and ducks flying by until 'Stop the bus!' Mr Weazley cried, 'I left my teeth on the mantelpiece.'
'Never you mind,' they said. 'You're not going to bite nobody,' and they gave him a bottle with a straw.
'I might want to smile,' he said.
'Not you,' they said . . . . .
'Twelve minutes to go,' shouted back the old man in the panama . . . .

The charabanc passes from pub to pub and Thomas moves easily and quickly from the robust comedy of the drinkers to the touching solitary musings of the boy. This exuberant tale, no doubt one of Thomas's most successful, certainly his most amusing and popular, was one of the last he wrote. It ends on a characteristic note of comic pathos:

And dusk came down warm and gentle on thirty, wild, wet, pickled, splashing men without a care in the world at the end of the world in the west of Wales.

These qualities of comedy and warm humanity have their final expression in *Under Milk Wood*. They, no doubt, account for its immediate and continued success; for it is probably the most regularly revived play of its time. Dylan Thomas's own rough manuscript sketch of the layout of Llaregyb indicates that its genesis was a small village by the sea, and he spoke of it as 'an extravagant play ... about a day's life in a small town in a never never Wales',[17] for though rooted in Laugharne it is essentially a work of the imagination. His letter about the play, written in 1951, is a fascinating account of its conception and of his compassionate attitude to its characters. That he conceived this work in terms of a particular place, Laugharne, is clearly shown in his sentence that the play is 'an impression for voices, an entertainment out of the darkness, of the town I live in'.[18] As the letter shows, Thomas accepts and understands the foibles of his characters, hinting at a basic innocence beneath all their eccentricities. Even Mr and Mrs Pugh, he says, are suited to each other, happy in their respective plotting and nagging. Though there are signs of the severe Nonconformist code in Jack Black's denunciations these only add to the 'pleasures of the little town wicked'. Evidently too, Thomas has a deep affection for Mary Ann Sailors' conviction that Llaregyb is the chosen land, 'she is not at all mad; she merely believes in heaven on earth'!

In his letter on *Under Milk Wood* Thomas indicates that he interprets and presents the life of the town on different levels of emotional truth, so that parody, irony and satire all have their part to play. Likewise, we *see* and *hear* the people who live their lives in this small sea town, their ordinariness and their goodness, like their eccentricities, not judged but explained and made 'strangely simple and simply strange' by the transforming power of the poet's imagination. It is one of those letters on whose composition Thomas spent much time and it remains the clearest and most rewarding critical comment on *Under Milk Wood*, so that it merits full quotation:

But out of my working, however vainly, on it, came the idea of Llareggub ... Out of it came the idea that I write a piece, a play, an impression for voices, an entertainment out of the darkness, of the town I live in, and to write it simply and warmly and comically with lots of movement and varieties of moods, so that, at many levels, through sight and speech, description and dialogue, evocation and parody, you come to know the town as an inhabitant of it ...

Let me particularize, and at random. As the piece goes on two voices will be predominant: that of the preacher, who talks only in verse, and that of the anonymous exhibitor and chronicler called, simply, First Voice. And the First Voice is really a kind of conscience, a guardian angel. Through him you will

Plate 48. At the Boat House overlooking the estuary.

learn about Mr Edwards, the draper, and Miss Price, the sempstress and their odd and, once it is made clear, most natural love. Every day of the week they write love letters to each other, he from the top, she from the bottom, of the town: all their lives they have known of each other's existence, and of their mutual love: they have seen each other a thousand times, and never spoken: easily they could have been together, married, had children: but that is not the life for them: their passionate love, at just this distance, is all they need. And Dai Bread, the baker, who has two wives: one is loving and mothering, sacklike and jolly: the other is gypsy slatternly and, all in love, hating: all three enjoy it. And Mrs Ogmore-Pritchard who, although a boarding house keeper, will keep no boarders because they cannot live up to the scrupulous and godlike tidiness of her house and because death can be the only boarder good enough for her in the end. And Mr Pugh, the schoolmaster, who is always nagged by his wife and who is always plotting her murder. This is well known to the town, and to Mrs Pugh. She likes nagging; he likes plotting, in supposed secrecy, against her. He would always like plotting, whoever he lived with; she would always like nagging, whoever she lived with. How lucky they are to be married. And Polly Garter has many illegitimate babies because she loves babies but does not want only one man's. And Cherry Owen the soak, who likes getting drunk every night; and his wife who likes living with two men, one sober in the day, one drunk at night. And the cobbler who thinks the town is the wickedest place to live in in the world, but who can never leave it while there is a hope of reforming it; and, oh, the savour his cries of Gomorrah add to the pleasures of the little town wicked. And the old woman who every morning shouts her age to the heavens; she believes the town is the chosen land, and the little river Dewi the River of Jordan; she is not at all mad: she merely believes in heaven on earth. And so with all of them, all the eccentrics whose eccentricities, in these first pages, are but briefly and impressionistically noted: all by their own rights are ordinary and good; and the First Voice, and the poet preacher, never judge nor condemn but explain and make strangely simple and simply strange.[19]

As the play developed, of course, the First and Second voices became the chroniclers and the voice of the preacher became the character Eli Jenkins, with his 'bardic' verses and his innocent and disarming comments on 'the little town wicked'.

The seed of the play is undoubtedly the broadcast talk *Quite Early One Morning* based topographically on New Quay and written during the year Thomas lived there. It is said that out in the bay, beyond the reef where the 'splashed' church of St Ina now stands at Llanina, only a few fields away from Majoda, Thomas's cliffside New Quay home, lies a drowned church and cemetery. Interestingly, when writing to Vernon Watkins about Majoda, Thomas stated that 'it's in a really wonderful bit of the bay, with a beach of its own'[20] – confirming the exact location of St Ina.[21] I think it likely that this story of a sea-drowned cemetery remained in Thomas's imagination, for the idea of a bell

Plate 49. The reef and bay at Llanina, New Quay, legendary site of the submerged graveyard.

tolling beneath the waves and a graveyard on the ocean bed is certainly a haunting one. We may recall, therefore, that *Under Milk Wood* opens with the voices of 'the long drowned' and the dead remembering the joys of life. Captain Cat dreams not of seas he sailed but seas the dead voyage in:

Captain Cat . . . dreams of

Second Voice: never such seas as any that swamped the decks of his *S.S.Kid-welly* bellying over the bedclothes and jellyfish-slippery sucking him down salt deep into the Davy dark where the fish come biting out and nibble him down to his wishbone, and the long drowned nuzzle up to him.

First Drowned: Remember me, Captain?

Captain Cat: You're Dancing Williams!

First Drowned: I lost my step in Nantucket.

Second Drowned: Do you see me, Captain? the white bone talking? I'm Tom-Fred the donkeyman . . . we shared the same girl once . . . her name was Mrs Probert . . .

Woman's Voice: Rosie Probert, thirty three Duck Lane. Come on up boys, I'm dead.

Third Drowned: Hold me, Captain, I'm Jonah Jarvis, come to a bad end, very enjoyable.

Fourth Drowned: Alfred Pomeroy Jones, sea-lawyer, born in Mumbles, sung like a linnet, crowned you with a flagon, tattooed with mermaids, thirst like a dredger, died of blisters.

First Drowned: This skull at your earhole is . . .

Fifth Drowned: Curly Bevan. Tell my auntie it was me that pawned the ormolu clock.

At the end of the play, as evening becomes night, 'the lights of the lamps in the windows call back the day and the dead that have run away to sea' and blind Captain Cat who now 'like a cat . . . sees in the dark . . . sails to see the dead.' It would seem that the story of the drowned cemetery is the literal truth that inspired the imaginative and poetic truth of Thomas's play.

It is surprising that the unusual name *Under Milk Wood* has aroused so little comment, for as the play moved to completion Thomas, so rightly, preferred the name to the original *Llareggub*. I think the name derives, in part, from Thomas's conception of his unfinished long poem *In Country Heaven*, for *Under Milk Wood* is imaginatively close to the natural landscapes and spiritual ethos from which the poetry is woven. Speaking of *In Country Heaven* Thomas referred to 'The god-head, the author, the milky-way farmer . . . He, on top of a hill in heaven';[22] and the natural world of Milk Wood has something of this 'milky-way' radiance and holiness, while its inhabitants share something

Plate 50. The present church at Llanina.

of the 'Edenie hearts'[14] of those living *In Country Heaven.*

I think, too, there is a literal base to the imaginative truth, as is usually the case in Dylan Thomas's writing. For facing Thomas, as he looked from his 'tree room on the cliff' or walked the cliff path to the village, was Sir John's Hill. On its lower slopes, meeting the estuary and mud flats, there is a wooded dingle; and above this, rich green fields where cows graze. A path leads from the shore through the narrow dingle past a now ruined byre, where to the left there are the fields, which inhabitants of Laugharne say have held milking-cows for generations past. And, significantly, a farm on the far side of the hill is called 'Salt House Farm' which must be the origin of the name 'Salt Lake Farm' in the play, and which Dylan drew on 'Llareggub Hill' in his sketch of the play's location. Looking at Sir John's Hill from Dylan's vantage point on the cliff path[23] or his shed, one sees how the hillside with its farm, fields, cows and 'green lathered trees' is the imaginative and actual setting of 'Milk Wood'. The town itself (with its

Plate 51. Laugharne and Sir John's Hill.

groups of lower and upper houses, just as in the play), its streets descending to the mud-flats and estuary at the foot of the hill, is literally below ('Under') Milk Wood.

Thomas's sketch of the setting of the play corresponds with the topography of Laugharne, but in mirror image.[24] He places the sea to the right, whereas in reality it is to the left (looking from the Boat House); the relationship of the lower and upper parts of the town is in reality the other way round, as is the direction of 'Coronation Street' (surely King Street?) where Brown's Hotel ('Sailor's Arms') is actually to the right of the Town Hall with its clock.

His sketch includes the lovers' lane, named *Goosegog Lane* – immediately recalling 'the grassgreen gooseberried double bed of the wood' that so excites the snooping Jack Black; and this lane Thomas locates on Llareggub (Sir John's) Hill, where there is indeed a courters' lane. Again, therefore, we remember the lines 'courters'-and-rabbits' wood limping invisible down to the ... crowblack, fishing boat-bobbing sea' that opens the play. It is well to bear in mind, too, that the phrase 'the gooseberry wood' first occurs in the opening stanza of Thomas's Rabelaisian poem *Lament*, that he described as 'coarse and violent',[25] written in 1951 when Thomas was working on *Under Milk Wood*. *Lament* tells the lecherous story of a 'windy boy'; reviled by the 'chapel fold' this black sheep (spit) recalls his sexual career with a comic verve and gift of characterization in verse that is clearly related to *Under Milk Wood*:

> When I was a windy boy and a bit
> And the black spit of the chapel fold,
> (Sighed the old ram rod, dying of women),

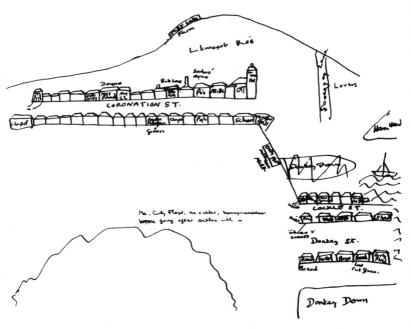

Plate 52. Dylan's sketch of 'Llareggub'.

119

> I tiptoed shy in the gooseberry wood,
> The rude owl cried like a telltale tit,
> I skipped in a blush as the big girls rolled
> Ninepin down on the donkeys' common,
> And on seesaw Sunday nights I wooed
> Whoever I would with my wicked eyes.

The word 'gooseberry' suggests of course the gooseberry bushes under which babies are said to be found.

Clearly 'Milk Wood' as place-name and title, has connotations of sexuality and fertility. And while in the children's teasing song the girl may be kissed 'in Goosegog Lane' and 'on Llaregyb Hill', the invitation to kiss her 'in Milk Wood' goes too far and is refused despite charges of 'cowardy cowardy custard'! It is important to remember that while to Mary Ann Sailors Milk Wood is a 'God-built garden' and to Eli Jenkins 'a greenleaved sermon on the innocence of men', it is also 'the fairday farmhands' wantoning ignorant chapel of bridesbeds' and to Jack Black 'hunters of lovers' its 'every tree-foot's cloven', for Pan and the devil haunt its milky-ways!

The whole setting is imaginatively 'a country heaven'. We may recall Dylan Thomas's words that when 'the Godhead ... the milky-way farmer ... on top of a hill in heaven ... weeps ... bushes and owls blow out like candles ... and the countrymen of heaven crouch all together under the hedges ... among themselves in the tear-salt darkness.'[22] Significantly, the play begins with the darkness of night and the drowned dead and returns to this at the close. The poem *Over Sir John's Hill* is of course part of the projected *In Country Heaven* sequence. It could be said of *Under Milk Wood*, as Thomas said of *In Country Heaven*, 'It grows into a praise of what is and what could be on this lump in the skies. It is a poem about happiness.'[26]

That Dylan Thomas had in mind the view of Sir John's Hill seems likely from his descriptions of the farm and Llaregyb Hill:

First Voice: He (NoGood Boyo sailing in the bay) turns his head and looks up at Llaregyb Hill, and sees, among green lathered trees, the white houses of the strewn away farms, where farmboys whistle, dogs shout, cows low, but all too far away for him, or you, to hear.

And again: Farmer Watkins in Salt Lake Farm hates his cattle on the hill as he ho's them in to milking.

While, with similar topographical precision, 'Bessie milks the lake-eyed cows as dusk showers slowly down over byre, sea and town'; for this almost palpable falling of twilight on hillside, estuary and village

Plate 53. Laugharne.

Dylan Thomas must have often observed from his cliffside vantage point.

The use of names and specific locations from Laugharne gives the play's poetry a particular base and inspiration. Manchester House, for instance, is a real shop in King Street. Further, there are actual 'Rose Cottage' and 'Bay View' named houses in Laugharne; interestingly 'trig and trim Bay View' is indeed 'at the top of the town', with its 'sea-view doors', being the last house on the cliff path before the Boat House. There is also a butcher's shop in nearby St Clear's called Eynon.[27] ('Butcher Beynon' . . .) There is little doubt that the Town Hall, with its clock-tower, in Market Street, Laugharne, supplied Thomas with a central point for Milk Wood, realistically and imaginatively; the clock in particular appealed to his sense of time and mutability, reflected in the twenty-four hour, cyclical, structure of the play. In this way the Town Hall, with its clock-tower, chiming bell, and weather cock furnishes Thomas with aptly used detail of sight and sound.

The path which led from Boat House to King Street (a five minutes' walk) passed a chapel and graveyard which are a short distance from the ivy-clad ruined castle. It seems, therefore, that such lines as 'An owl flies home past Bethesda to a chapel in an oak' were based on the poet's observation as he walked this path at night. His evening drinking at Brown's Hotel might likewise have inspired the surreal comedy of Organ Morgan who 'goes to chapel to play the organ' and mistakes 'Cherry Owen who is resting on a tombstone on his way home' for 'Bach lying on a tombstone'.

I make these points to indicate how Thomas's imaginative fantasy, his gift for comic and poetic inventiveness were not, as is often supposed, fanciful persiflage, but rooted in particularity and locality. Thus, with humorous accuracy, the 'Voice of a Guide-Book' notes the small pink-washed two-storey houses that crowd the lower sea-end of the town, while the upper part of Laugharne's main street boasts Georgian houses 'of more pretension, if, on the whole, in a sad state of repair'. Another instance of the literal base of much of Thomas's writing lies in the evocation of Evans the Death who:

sees, upon waking fifty years ago, snow lie deep on the goosefield behind the sleeping house; and he runs out into the field where his mother is making welshcakes in the snow, and steals a fistful of snowflakes and currants and climbs back to bed to eat them cold and sweet under the warm, white clothes while his mother dances in the snow kitchen crying out for her lost currants.

It was the custom in Wales to use snow in the making of welshcakes (thick biscuit-like cakes), which gave them an exquisite lightness. It is also a matter of literary interest that the Rev. Eli Jenkins' lines:

> A tiny dingle is Milk Wood
> By Golden Grove 'neath Grongar

commemorate the village Golden Grove, and the hill Grongar Hill, both near Llandeilo, to the north-east of Carmarthen in the direction of Llangadog. Grongar Hill is celebrated in John Dyer's poem of that name, an eighteenth century 'place' poem. Dyer was from this area, and was a poet, like Thomas, deeply responsive to nature. Finally, one might add that in the reference to *The White Book of Llaregyb* in Milk Wood, Thomas is possibly echoing the *White Book of Rhydderch*,[28] a precious manuscript collection of old Welsh tales, which were – with the *Red Book of Hergest* – collected and translated under the title of *Mabinogion*. Thomas must have known some of these stories for he refers to

King Arthur, linking him with Laugharne; and we may guess that in his father's library in Cwmdonkin Drive there may have been a copy of the Charlotte Guest *Mabinogion*, published in the Everyman edition in 1906. And interestingly, in December 1952, Thomas had arranged to prepare a collection of Welsh fairy tales and legends for Oxford University Press.

Thomas had learned by this time to make full use of Welsh literary and social traditions. For example, the Reverend Eli Jenkins' description of 'Llaregyb Hill, that mystic tumulus, the memorial of peoples that dwelt in the region of Llaregyb before the Celts left the Land of Summer and where the old wizards made themselves a wife out of flowers', echoes a passage in Gwyn Jones's book *A Prospect of Wales* (published in 1948 – close to the time of writing *Under Milk Wood*): 'As soon as I saw anything I saw Twm Barlwm, that mystic tumulus, the memorial of peoples that dwelt in that region before the Celts left the Land of Summer.'[29] Dylan Thomas's reference to the creation of a wife out of flowers has its source in the *Mabinogion:*

'Well,' said Math, 'we will seek, I and thou, by charms and illusion, to form a wife for him out of flowers' ... So they took the blossoms of the oak, and the blossoms of the broom, and the blossoms of the meadow-sweet, and produced from them a maiden, the fairest and most graceful that man ever saw. And they baptized her, and gave her the name of Blodeuwedd.[30]

The Reverend Eli Jenkins is Thomas's most kindly portrait of a Welsh minister, and his innocent comment on hearing Polly Garter's song of sexual reminiscence illustrates both the irony and assured modulation of feeling in the play:

> I loved a man whose name was Tom
> He was strong as a bear and two yards long
> I loved a man whose name was Dick
> He was big as a barrel and three feet thick
> And I loved a man whose name was Harry
> Six feet tall and sweet as a cherry ...

> Rev. Eli Jenkins: Praise the Lord! We are a musical nation.

Of course a vein of lewd comedy salts the play; songs and words having a *double entente*. The characters express their feelings with a disarming and generally comic frankness, which shocked some at the time, but has retained its freshness. Gossamer Beynon does not care if Sinbad Sailors is common, 'I want to gobble him up. I don't care if he *does* drop his aitches . . . . so long as he's all cucumber and hooves.'

Plate 54. In the garden of the Boat House.

Mae Rose Cottage 'listens to the nanny goats chew, draws circles of lipstick round her nipples' and confides to the unlistening goats, 'I'm fast. I'm a bad lot. God will strike me dead. I'm seventeen. I'll go to hell . . . . I'll sin till I blow up' and 'lies deep, waiting for the worst to happen.' Equally obsessed, Jack Black nightly 'climbs into his religious trousers, their flies sewn up with cobbler's thread, and pads out, torched and bibled, grimly, joyfully, into the already sinning dusk!' Certain words, such as 'martyr', 'music', recur as sexual puns: – 'Saint Polly Garter,' exclaims a gossip. 'She was martyred again last night,' while Mrs Organ Morgan laments, 'Oh, I'm a martyr to music.'

Bearing in mind the static and unadventurous nature of dramatic writing at this time – for it was four years before the revival and flowering of the English theatre that began in 1956 – it is clear that Thomas was innovative in the colloquial vitality and sexual jests of his comedy, in his use of song to create the atmosphere and assist the changing moods of the play, and in the freedom and novelty of his technique. Invited to write a play for radio, he wrote 'a play for voices' which, instead of following customary forms, took the opportunities for an original and imaginative dramatic structure that depended on the full exploitation of the possibilities of language. Language, via apt selection of metaphor and image, is used to evoke the scene, whether the village asleep at night or at its morning chores; to create character, e.g. Jack Black, Mae Rose Cottage; and to convey the passing of time. There is no plot, no action, no development of incident, for time sequence has taken the place of narrative sequence, and the form of the play is the passage of one day in the lives of the inhabitants of the village. Part of Thomas's command of language is his command of rhythm, and it is essentially a poetic drama. The first and second voice, like all-seeing television cameras, spot and bring on stage the people of this village. Significantly, too, the play opens with the dead remembering the sweetness of life; and rhythm and phrase, especially in the dialogue, belong essentially to the South Wales dialect of English:

> First Drowned: How's it above?
> Second Drowned: Is there rum and laverbread? . . .
> First Drowned: Fighting and onions?
> Second Drowned: And sparrows and daisies?
> Third Drowned: Tiddlers in a jamjar? . . .
> First Drowned: Washing on the line?
> Second Drowned: And old girls in the snug?
> Third Drowned: How's the tenors in Dowlais?
> Fourth Drowned: Who milks the cows in Maesgwyn?

The use of sacramental imagery to describe the natural world recalls the world of the later poetry. *Under Milk Wood* is imaginatively close to *In Country Heaven*, for the poet is celebrating 'the innocence of men' and the 'kind fire' of God in 'this place of love'. And undoubtedly it is blind Captain Cat's cry, 'Come back, come back', that is the dominant note of the play and its 'remembered tellings'. As Polly Garter makes love, it is for a dead lover she longs:

> But I always think as we tumble into bed
> Of Little Willy Wee who is dead, dead, dead . . . . .

Often nostalgic reflection is veined both with pathos and comedy:

Alone until she dies, Bessie Bighead . . . picks a posy of daisies in Sunday Meadow to put on the grave of Gomer Owen who kissed her once by the pigsty when she wasn't looking and never kissed her again although she was looking all the time.

But there is, too, a seriousness on the subject of death as profound and haunting as that in the poetry, as in dead Rosie Probert's metamorphosis:

> Remember her.
> She is forgetting.
> The earth which filled her mouth
> Is vanishing from her.
> Remember me.
> I have forgotten you.
> I am going into the darkness of the darkness for ever.
> I have forgotten that I was ever born.

Less than a month after completing the play, Dylan Thomas died, in New York, on 9 November 1953, while on his fourth American lecture tour. Had Dylan Thomas remained in Laugharne and not undertaken that ill-presaged fourth and final tour – undertaken against the advice and deepest instincts of both his wife and his mother – then he would have had the daily care and love of his family and close, not simply casual, friends. At a time when it would seem he was particularly vulnerable, both physically and emotionally, this support was vital. It is well to remember his father had not long died, a grief that must have deeply torn him as a man and which was tearing fiercely mourning poems from him. Just before this final visit to America he had suffered blackouts; on one occasion collapsing while at a cinema in Carmarthen, on another in Brown's Hotel.

Thomas had a wife and three children to keep, with no regular income, and these last years were harassed by lack of money. Demands

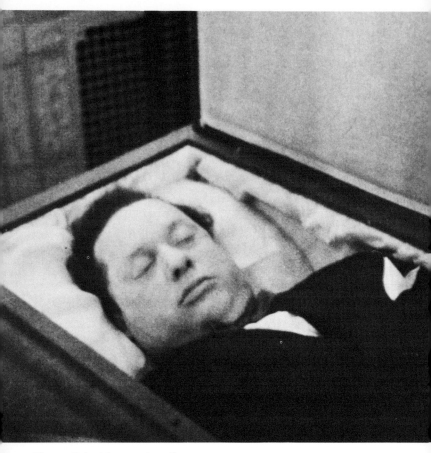

Plate 55. Dylan Thomas in his coffin.

for long standing tax debts created a financial crisis, and the American tours were originally undertaken as a means of earning quickly large sums of money to pay these debts. The emotional and physical toll these tours made on a man not in good health, proved unendurable. In Wales he usually drank beer, regularly but not to excess. In America the strain of the tours made the proffered whiskies all too irresistible, the bouts of hard drinking a flight from loneliness and exhaustion, despite the lionizing he enjoyed. 'For Dylan,' writes his wife, '. . . this (America) was a poisonous atmosphere: he needed opposition, gentle, but firm, constant curbing. Nobody ever needed encouragement less, and he was drowned in it.'³¹

Of course his achievement as a reader was that Dylan Thomas established the popularity of poetry with large audiences: his records and broadcasts were to continue this. Due to the passionate eloquence of his recitals he brought poetry from the stuffy, captive, and all-too-cerebral worlds of lecture room, literary salon, and self-regarding clique, whether cosmopolitan or provincial. He was in the tradition of Dickens in his gift for popularization of the art he practised by the power and authority of his reading and personality. But this was at a cost to himself, for he spurned the careful, measured, and self protective style of the professional lecturer. Thomas was as profligate of his gifts as a reader as he was also of all things material. Caitlin Thomas, who accompanied him on one of the tours, records how 'he gave to those wide-open-beaked readings the concentrated artillery of his flesh and blood, and, above all, his breath. I used to come in late and hear, through the mikes, the breath – straining, panting.'³²

Then there were those gruesome academic gatherings/parties that followed the readings, the insensitive (and often not very intelligent) questioning of the captive poet, the pedagogic longueurs, the impertinent

Plate 56. The funeral.

demands for his already exhausted attention. It is no wonder that he was driven to drink and rude comment. But more destructive still was the loneliness, homesickness, and sense of isolation. Perhaps not surprisingly, an earlier tour seems to have resulted in a brief love affair. And this of course added to the personal and family tensions.

However, despite the many problems of these last years, all contributing their share of anguish and worry, despite the cumulative fatigue of American tours, Dylan Thomas's creative powers were undiminished, breaking new ground, as I have shown, in the poems and *Under Milk Wood*. With publication of *Collected Poems* in November 1952, Thomas was spoken of as 'the greatest living poet'[33] in English, and the book was an immediate best-seller. Ironically, the tide of his finances was about to turn, for *Under Milk Wood*, another best-seller, was soon to be published.

As Caitlin Thomas makes abundantly clear, in Laugharne Dylan Thomas had the 'steady dull, homely bed of straw to breed his fantasies in',[32] where the five hour daily dedication to his 'craft and sullen art' was not interrupted by the need to play the poet. In a broadcast on 5 November 1953, Thomas, for the last time, with love and affectionate humour, told of 'this timeless, mild, beguiling island of a town with its seven public-houses, one chapel in action, the church, one factory, two billiard tables, one St Bernard (without Brandy), one policeman, three rivers, a visiting sea . . .'[34] It was during this broadcast from Laugharne's school hall that his wife received news that her husband was 'lying unconscious in an American hospital'.[35]

Shortly before his death Thomas spoke of his longing for Wales and home: 'He opened his eyes and, calmly, sadly, said: "Tonight in my home the men have their arms round one another, and they are singing"'[36] He was thinking of the familiar Welsh Saturday evening in the pub, evenings he had spent in Laugharne, in Brown's or the Cross Inn, a short walk from his 'sea-shaken' home.

Undoubtedly Thomas was not in good health when he set out for his tour; undoubtedly it was to exhaust him further; but it seems now that a contributory factor to the circumstances of Dylan Thomas's tragic and untimely death in New York was medical error. Certainly the suggestions that he wished to die, that his genius was spent, are falsifying legend. The now famous poem written for his dying father rings with a personal cry against death, invoking the light that shines through

Plate 57. The grave in Laugharne churchyard.

his last poems. This is not poetry of failing inspiration, but the voice of
the lyric poet passionately learning to grow old:

> And you, my father, there on the sad height,
> Curse, bless me, now with your fierce tears, I pray.
> Do not go gentle into that good night.
> Rage, rage against the dying of the light.

Plate 58. Cwmdonkin Park.

Bibliography

This bibliography lists books referred to or used in connection with the present study.

Works by Dylan Thomas:
Books
18 Poems, London, 1934.
Twenty-Five Poems, London, 1936.
The Map of Love, London, 1939.
Portrait of the Artist as a Young Dog, London, 1940.
Deaths and Entrances, London, 1946.
Collected Poems, London, 1952.
Under Milk Wood, London, 1954.
Quite Early One Morning, London, 1954.
A Prospect of the Sea, London, 1955.
Adventures in the Skin Trade and Other Stories, New York, 1955.
Letters to Vernon Watkins (ed. Vernon Watkins), London, 1957.
Selected Letters of Dylan Thomas (ed. Constantine Fitzgibbon),
    London, 1966.
Poet in the Making: The Notebooks of Dylan Thomas (ed. R. Maud),
    London, 1968.
Dylan Thomas: The Poems (ed. Daniel Jones), London, 1971.
Dylan Thomas: Early Prose Writings (ed. Walford Davies), London,
    1971.

Articles (referred to in the text)
'Children's Hour', *Swansea Grammar School Magazine*, vol. 27, no. 3,
    pp. 87–9.
'A Modern Poet of Gower: Anglo-Welsh Bards', *Herald of Wales*
    (25 June 1932), p. 8.
'Poetic Manifesto', *Texas Quarterly*, vol. 4, no. 4 (Winter 1961). Also

published in *Dylan Thomas: Early Prose Writings* and in Andrew Sinclair, *Dylan Thomas*.

Standard bibliographies:
J. Alexander Rolph: *Dylan Thomas: A Bibliography*, London, 1956.
Ralph Maud: *Dylan Thomas in Print: A Bibliographical History*, London, 1970.

Works about Dylan Thomas:
Books
Brinnin, J.M.: *Dylan Thomas in America*, London, 1956.
Thomas, Caitlin: *Leftover Life to Kill*, London, 1957.
Ackerman, John: *Dylan Thomas: His Life and Work*, London, 1964.
Read, Bill: *The Days of Dylan Thomas*, London, 1964.
Fitzgibbon, Constantine: *The Life of Dylan Thomas*, London, 1965.
Cleverdon, Douglas: *The Growth of Milk Wood*, London, 1969.
Davies, Walford: *Dylan Thomas* (Writers of Wales, University of Wales Press, 1972).
Ackerman, John: *Welsh Dylan:* Catalogue of Welsh Arts Council Exhibition on Dylan Thomas prepared by present author, 1973.
Sinclair, Andrew: *Dylan Thomas: Poet of his People*, London, 1975.
Ferris, Paul: *Dylan Thomas,* London, 1977.
Jones, Daniel: *My Friend Dylan Thomas*, London, 1977.

Articles
Ackerman, John: 'Dylan Thomas' in *Encyclopaedia Britannica* (1966 edition).
Ackerman, John: Review Article in *The Anglo-Welsh Review*, vol. 20, no. 46, pp. 175–81.
Ackerman, John: 'The Role of Nature in the Poetry of Dylan Thomas' in *Triskel Two* (ed. Adams and Hughes), Christopher Davies, 1973.
Ackerman, John: Review in *Poetry Wales*, vol. 13, no. 4, pp. 120–25.
Dodsworth, Martin: 'The Concept of Mind and the Poetry of Dylan Thomas' in *New Critical Essays* (ed. Walford Davies), Dent, 1972, pp. 107–35.
Jones, Gwyn: 'Welsh Dylan', *Adelphi*, vol. 30, no. 2 (February 1954), pp. 108–17. I am indebted to Professor Gwyn Jones's article for the title of this book.

Moore, Geoffrey: 'Dylan Thomas', *Kenyon Review*, vol. xvii, no. 2 (Spring 1955), pp. 258–79.

Watkins, Vernon: Introduction to *Letters to Vernon Watkins*, London, 1957, pp. 11–21.

Notes

Part I: Swansea and the early years: 1914–1934: Growth of the Poet.

1. Dylan Thomas: quoted by Geoffrey Moore in 'Dylan Thomas', *Kenyon Review*, vol. xvii (Spring 1955), p. 261.
2. Dylan Thomas: 'Reminiscences of Childhood', *Quite Early One Morning*, pp. 1–7.
3. Edward Thomas: *The Life and Letters of Edward Thomas* (ed. John Moore, London 1939), pp. 156 and 168.
4. Dylan Thomas: 'Holiday Memory', *Quite Early One Morning*, p. 31.
5. Dylan Thomas: *Selected Letters of Dylan Thomas* (ed. Constantine Fitzgibbon), p. 52.
6. Mrs D. J. Thomas: in an interview reported in *Everybody's* (21 April 1956), pp. 23 and 39. The article, entitled 'Go and Write, Boy!', was written by Paul Ferris.
7. Dylan Thomas: *Selected Letters of Dylan Thomas* (ed. Constantine Fitzgibbon), p. 78.
8. Dylan Thomas: *Letters to Vernon Watkins*, p. 104.
9. *The Mabinogion*, translated by Lady Charlotte Guest, facsimile edition, John Jones (Cardiff 1977), p. 421.
10. Dylan Thomas: *Selected Letters of Dylan Thomas* (ed. Constantine Fitzgibbon), p. 23.
11. Dylan Thomas: 'The Fight', *Portrait of the Artist as a Young Dog*, p. 77.
12. Dylan Thomas: *Letters to Vernon Watkins*, p. 54.
13. Dylan Thomas: *Poet In The Making: The Notebooks of Dylan Thomas* (ed. R. Maud), p. 155.
14. Daniel Jones: *Dylan Thomas: The Poems* (ed. Daniel Jones), p. 271.
15. Dylan Thomas: 'Return Journey', *Quite Early One Morning*, p. 85.
16. Dylan Thomas: *Swansea Grammar School Magazine*, vol. 27, no. 3 (December 1930), pp. 87–9.
17. Review in *Swansea Grammar School Magazine*, vol. 27, no. 1.
18. Review in *Swansea Grammar School Magazine*, vol. 27, no. 4 (April 1931).
19. *Swansea Grammar School Magazine*, vol. 27, no. 3 (December 1930), p. 112.
20. Dylan Thomas: 'Return Journey', *Quite Early One Morning*, pp. 80–81.
21. Dylan Thomas: 'A Modern Poet of Gower: Anglo-Welsh Bards', *Herald of Wales* (25 June 1932), p. 8.
22. Dylan Thomas: 'Old Garbo', *Portrait of the Artist as a Young Dog*, pp. 195–6.
23. Dylan Thomas: *Selected Letters of Dylan Thomas* (ed. Constantine Fitzgibbon), p. 27.
24. Ibid. p. 4 and p. 3. 'Oystered' is a characteristic Thomas pun, for the village of Oystermouth begins the Mumbles seascape, linking Mumbles and Swansea.
25. Ibid., pp. 26–7.
26. Ibid., p. 43.
27. Dylan Thomas: *Letters to Vernon Watkins*, p. 47.
28. Dylan Thomas: *Selected Letters of Dylan Thomas* (ed. Fitzgibbon), p. 17.

29. Ibid., p. 126 and p. 127.
30. Ibid., p. 40.
31. Ibid., pp. 63–4.
32. Vernon Watkins: 'Introduction', *Letters to Vernon Watkins*, pp. 12–13.
33. Dylan Thomas: 'Return Journey', *Quite Early One Morning*, p. 82.
34. Dylan Thomas: 'One Warm Saturday', *Portrait of the Artist as a Young Dog*, p. 217.
35. Dylan Thomas: *Selected Letters of Dylan Thomas* (ed. Fitzgibbon), p. 18.
36. Ibid., p. 204.
37. Ibid., p. 47.
38. Ibid., p. 48.
39. Ibid., p. 87.
40. William Blake: *Poetry and Prose* (ed. G. Keynes, London 1946), p. 187.
41. Dylan Thomas: *Selected Letters of Dylan Thomas* (ed. Fitzgibbon), p. 23.
42. Stephen Spender: *Spectator* (5 December 1952), pp. 780–1.
43. Dylan Thomas: *Selected Letters of Dylan Thomas* (ed. Fitzgibbon), p. 386.
44. Gwyn Jones: Introduction to *Welsh Short Stories* (London 1956), p. xiii.
45. Gwyn Jones: 'Welsh Dylan', *Adelphi*, vol. 30, no. 2 (February 1954), p. 115.
46. Dylan Thomas: quoted in *Adam*, no. 238 (December 1953), p. 68.
47. Dylan Thomas: *Selected Letters of Dylan Thomas* (ed. Fitzgibbon), p. 143.
48. Dylan Thomas: 'Return Journey', *Quite Early One Morning*, pp. 75–6.
49. Dylan Thomas: quoted in *Adam*, no. 238, p. 68.

Part II: Exile and Return Journeys: 1934–1949.

1. Dylan Thomas: 'A Painter's Studio', *Texas Quarterly* (Winter 1961), pp. 56–7.
2. Dylan Thomas: *Selected Letters* (ed. Fitzgibbon), pp. 147–8.
3. Dylan Thomas: *Letters to Vernon Watkins*, p. 49.
4. Dylan Thomas: *Selected Letters* (ed. Fitzgibbon), p. 48.
5. Dylan Thomas: *Letters to Vernon Watkins*, p. 27.
6. Dylan Thomas: *Selected Letters* (ed. Fitzgibbon), p. 195.
7. Ibid., pp. 200–201.
8. Ibid., p. 205.
9. Ibid., p. 240.
10. Dylan Thomas: *Letters to Vernon Watkins*, p. 50.
11. Gwyn Jones: 'Welsh Dylan', *Adelphi*, vol. 30, no. 2 (February 1954), p. 115.
12. P. B. Shelley: 'Adonais', *Complete Poetical Works* (ed. T. Hutchinson, O.U.P. 1952), p. 441.
13. Dylan Thomas: *The Poems* (ed. Daniel Jones), p. 179.
14. Dylan Thomas in a letter from Gelli, Talsarn. *Selected Letters* (ed. Fitzgibbon), p. 259.
15. Dylan Thomas: 'Three Poems', *Quite Early One Morning*, p. 157.

Part III: Fern Hill and Childhood.

1. Dylan Thomas: *Collected Poems*, p. 163.
2. Dylan Thomas: 'On Reading One's Own Poems', *Quite Early One Morning*, p. 137.
3. Dylan Thomas: *Selected Letters* (ed. Fitzgibbon), p. 11.
4. Dylan Thomas: *Poet In The Making: The Notebooks of Dylan Thomas* (ed. R. Maud), p. 168.
5. Dylan Thomas: *Letters to Vernon Watkins*, p. 58.
6. Dylan Thomas: quoted by Constantine Fitzgibbon in *The Life of Dylan Thomas*, p. 281.
7. Dylan Thomas: quoted in *Dylan Thomas* by Paul Ferris, p. 45.
8. Vernon Watkins: 'Introduction' to *Letters to Vernon Watkins*, p. 13.

9. Dylan Thomas: *Letters to Vernon Watkins*, p. 104.
10. Thomas Traherne: *Centuries of Meditations*, p. 157.
11. Henry Vaughan: 'The Retreat', *The Works of Henry Vaughan*, vol. 1 (ed. L. C. Martin, 1957), pp. 419–20.
12. W. B. Yeats in 'Letter to his father', July 1913. *The Letters of W. B. Yeats* (ed. Allan Wade, 1954), p. 583.
13. Dylan Thomas: *Selected Letters* (ed. Fitzgibbon), pp. 24 and 25.
14. Dylan Thomas: 'Three Poems', *Quite Early One Morning*, p. 157.
15. Dylan Thomas: *Letters to Vernon Watkins*, p. 131.
16. Dylan Thomas: *Selected Letters* (ed. Fitzgibbon), p. 35.
17. Ibid., pp. 278–9.
18. Dylan Thomas: *Letters to Vernon Watkins*, p. 114.
19. Ibid., p. 116.
20. Dylan Thomas: quoted by J. M. Brinnin: *Dylan Thomas in America*, p. 147.
21. Dylan Thomas: *Selected Letters* (ed. Fitzgibbon), pp. 234–5.
22. Confirmation of this use of the word is recorded in 'Spreading the Net: Survey of the Lore and Language of Welsh Fisher-Folk': Bill Bundy, *The Anglo-Welsh Review*, vol. 26, no. 59, p. 70.
23. William Wordsworth: 'Ode on Intimations of Immortality', *Poetical Works*, vol. 4 (O.U.P. 1947), p. 280.
24. Dylan Thomas: *Selected Letters* (ed. Fitzgibbon), p. 236.

Part IV: Laugharne: 'Druid in his own Land'.

1. Gwyn Jones: 'Welsh Dylan', *Adelphi*, vol. 30, no. 2 (February 1954), p. 115.
2. Dylan Thomas: *Selected Letters* (ed. Fitzgibbon), p. 29.
3. Ibid., p. 382.
4. W. B. Yeats: *Essays* (London 1924), p. 330.
5. Dylan Thomas: 'Three Poems', *Quite Early One Morning*, p. 158.
6. Dylan Thomas: from 'Poetic Manifesto', quoted in *Dylan Thomas* by Andrew Sinclair, p. 231.
7. W. B. Yeats: 'The Fisherman', *Collected Poems*, p. 167.
8. Caitlin Thomas: *Leftover Life to Kill*, p. 35.
9. Ibid., pp. 36–7.
10. This information is included in *Dylan Thomas* by Paul Ferris, p. 264.
11. Caitlin Thomas: *Empire News*, article on Dylan Thomas.
12. Dylan Thomas: quoted in *Dylan Thomas* by Andrew Sinclair, p. 156.
13. Dylan Thomas: 'Three Poems', *Quite Early One Morning*, p. 155.
14. Ibid., p. 157.
15. W. B. Yeats: *Collected Poems*, p. 278.
16. Ibid., p. 338.
17. Dylan Thomas: *Selected Letters* (ed. Fitzgibbon), p. 384.
18. Ibid., p. 364.
19. Ibid., pp. 364–5.
20. Dylan Thomas: *Letters to Vernon Watkins*, p. 115.
21. We read in the *Archaeologia Cambrensis 1846–1900* that in 1859 a Mr R. D. Jenkins 'knew that . . . it (the sea) had been gradually and continually gaining ground near Aberayron, at a place called Llanina, between the last mentioned place and New Quay . . . There was every reason to apprehend that it would not be very long before the parish church . . . of Llanina itself would be swept away.' *A.C.*, vol. 5 (Third Series) 1859, p. 339.
22. Dylan Thomas: 'Three Poems', *Quite Early One Morning*, p. 156.
23. I am indebted to Bernard Wiggins, curator of the Boat House, for the seed of this

idea when he pointed out to me the view of these fields on Sir John's Hill from the cliff path alongside Dylan Thomas's writing room on the cliff, a pastoral setting where cows grazed on fields whose green seemed to vary in shade with the changing light of the day, such was its luminosity from that vantage-point.

24. I am indebted for this interesting suggestion to John Idris Jones, publisher of the present book.
25. Dyland Thomas: *Selected Letters* (ed. Fitzgibbon), p. 353.
26. Dylan Thomas: 'Three Poems', *Quite Early One Morning*, p. 157.
27. I am again indebted to Bernard Wiggins who pointed this out to me.
28. I am indebted to John Idris Jones for this suggestion.
29. These words by Arthur Machen are quoted by Gwyn Jones: *A Prospect of Wales* (London 1948), p. 17.
30. *The Mabinogion*, translated by Lady Charlotte Guest, a facsimile edition, John Jones (Cardiff 1977), p. 426.
31. Caitlin Thomas: *Leftover Life to Kill, pp. 58–9.*
32. Ibid., p. 59.
33. Philip Toynbee in *Observer* review of *Collected Poems*, November 1952.
34. Dylan Thomas: 'Laugharne', *Quite Early One Morning*, p. 71.
35. A. T. Davies in 'Notes' to this broadcast, *Quite Early One Morning*, p. 176.
36. J. M. Brinnin: *Dylan Thomas in America*, p. 211.

Index

Note: figures in italics refer to photographs